Roberta

Roberta

Joy and Courage in a Clay Jar Too Soon Broken

By Charlene May

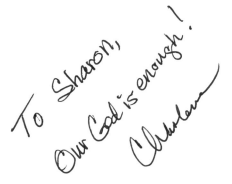

To Sharon,
Our God is enough!
Charlene

Roberta

Joy and courage in a Clay Jar Too Soon Broken

This is an attempt to capture the spirit of an amazing woman. To protect some people, and because others could not be reached to grant permission, I have not always used real names. Though most of it is true -- none of it is "made up" -- the memories of Roberta and others are the source for much of it. It should be read in that light.

ISBN: 9781695033450

TABLE OF CONTENTS

DEDICATION

To my husband, David, who has inspired and encouraged me to stretch and grow. His godliness is reflected in his vision. Thank you, Dave, for holding my hand these past 53 years as we walked through doors of adventure and uncertainty, yet with confidence that God's hand was closed over ours.

INTRODUCTION

I began writing this book in 2013. Shortly after moving to Haiti the previous year, I knew someone needed to write the story of Roberta. During the next couple of years, I sought out quiet moments with Roberta to learn of her life's journey --- the journey which brought her to Port au Prince, Haiti.

Working on the book in Punta Cuna, Dominican Republic

With financial help from a friend, David and I took Roberta for a week's getaway to the Dominican Republic in July 2015, just three months before her unexpected death. I had begun to feel an urgency about the book, but had no premonition how precious that week would become.

After an exhausted Roberta slept the entire two-day bus trip to Punta Cuna and the first two days at the resort, she was finally rested enough to talk "book". During the next four days, Roberta told me about the 36 children who had come to live with her during the past 20 years. One afternoon she looked up and said, "You know we're gonna have to write a second book, don't you?" The 2010 earthquake and its aftermath were such defining moments, she believed an entire book was required to tell its story.

Sadly, I never got the opportunity to hear what she most wanted to share about the earthquake, its effect on her family and on the country of Haiti.

Her sudden death on October 10, 2015, has necessitated reliance on my memory concerning many details. I contacted key people involved in her ministry but was unable to contact all involved. I've often wished I could call or text Roberta to clarify facts and information. When picking up my manuscript to resume writing after Roberta's death, tears filled my eyes as I changed present tense words into past tense.

Reliving the past 14 years of life with Roberta has been full of beautiful memories and an aching heart to hear her burst of laughter and witness her untiring example of ministry. This book has indeed been a work of love and I pray it is a tribute that will give God glory and Roberta honor.

I hesitate to put the finishing touches on the book and send it to the publisher --- it will be as though I am closing her casket. I have spent the greater part of this past year thinking about her, reliving our experiences together, and savoring our sweet friendship. I hate to let her go.

DISCLAIMERS

I ask for leniencies from those of you involved in various aspects of this ministry who will find inaccuracies or omittance of important events or people. I pray they will not blemish my intent to fairly and lovingly share Roberta's life story.

There is much information written about some of the children and little information on others. A few of Roberta's older children articulate easily, both verbally and in written form, and were better able to share their stories. Children with major health issues necessarily required more information and explanation.

In no way do I want to minimize the importance of each child and the contribution he or she made to the Sonlight family. Each child has a story worth telling and I have tried to give each one a voice, no matter how small. As the years went by, some of the children came and went without sharing their stories, either because they are private people or the language barrier was too great.

ACKNOWLEGEMENTS

It has taken a village to gather the contents of this book. I must thank, first, my husband David. Without his computer savvy and endless patience, there would be no book --- period. He spent endless hours preparing this manuscript for publication, exercising great restraint, endurance, and his sense of humor.

David May, Linda Lingo, Jesse Robertson, Jan Sharp, Wanda Shunk, Danna Pritchard, Traci Robinson, Glo Erickson, and Michael May --- there are no words to express my appreciation for the hours and energy you sacrificed to proofread and bring this book to the next level.

My special thanks to Widlord Thomas and Michemana Blaise for their help in filling in gaps concerning the 2010 earthquake and for sharing so much of their lives, enriching Roberta's story.

Much appreciation to Jesse Robertson, Larry Waymire, and Bobbie Solley, whose valuable contributions to the manuscript added insightful thoughts about Roberta's ministry.

PREAMBLE

God uses ordinary people to do extraordinary things. He used a runaway adopted son of an Egyptian Pharaoh to rescue His people from slavery; one faithful man to build an ark to save his family and animals before destroying the sinful world; a shepherd boy to become King of Israel; and a fisherman to become a spiritual giant in His new church. I would add Roberta's name to that list.

Roberta had been a Christian only four years when she began to feel called to relieve some of the suffering in Haiti, especially the suffering of children. She was young, single, childless, had never taught a Bible class, and spoke no Creole. From all outward appearances, she was not equipped to effectively minister to the people of Haiti. But God equips ordinary people to do extraordinary things.

After working with Roberta, I feel compelled to tell her story of how God first planted a seed of faith in Roberta, then watered and nurtured it with challenges, failures, and victories.

This is the remarkable story of how God used one woman to make grassroots changes in an impoverished and harsh country embedded with voodoo.

Roberta dared to say "yes" to God, following His call to minister to desperate people who would have a difficult time trusting and accepting her love.

She was murdered October 10, 2015.

Roberta's Family About 2015

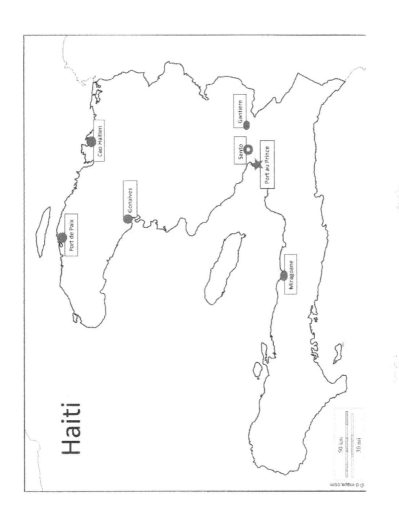

17

PROLOGUE

"Be careful --- there are men who will want to kill me."

These were the first words spoken by Roberta's husband as they disembarked the plane. Fear gripped her heart as Roberta walked the tarmac toward the airport.

Men scrambled and pushed, vying to get control of their luggage. Mass confusion reigned. Outside was worse than inside. The streets were filled with garbage and stench, sick people, and dead bodies --- evidence of President Aristide's latest embargo and his refusal of help offered by other world governments. He had recently lifted the embargo, but it would take months for this country to regain any sense of normalcy.

Thus was Roberta's introduction to Port-au-Prince, Haiti, in August 1995. Her life would be forever changed.

PART I
Training up a Missionary

"Parents can only give good advice or put them on the right paths, but the final forming of a person's character lies in their own hands."

- Anne Frank

Chapter 1
Elementary School

On January 26, 1960, Roberta (known as Bobbie throughout her childhood) was born in Honolulu, HI. A couple of years later, the family was completed with a baby boy.

Outside of her heavenly Father, Roberta's father was the single greatest influence in her life. He came up through the ranks of the United States Marine Corps, retiring as a Lt. Colonel. His integrity and high moral values enabled him to overcome the prejudices and unfair treatment that were his as a young black man.

He was an athlete, a mechanic, an accomplished soldier, an avid reader, a man of great wisdom. Bobbie loved her daddy and stayed near his elbow during her growing-up years. He didn't know it at the time, but he was preparing Roberta for living independently in a third world country. He taught her how to fix cars and plumbing. He taught her how to reason through a problem. He taught her to recognize the good and bad traits of people and how to love them anyway. He modeled how to take care of herself in a bigoted world, yet make peace along her way. He instilled in her bravery and courageousness --- never to be a quitter or settle for less.

Bobbie's mother was a strong woman with a good work ethic, an advocate for young black girls, and was an athlete in her own right. She was a stay-at-home mom and did a fantastic job transitioning the family in their numerous moves, acting as both mother and father during her husband's deployments.

Each move was a new adventure for Bobbie. Being an extrovert, she anticipated the fun of making new friends ---

learning what they liked to do and sharing experiences of their pasts. She enjoyed exploring new places, checking out what was different from the last place she called home.

Her parents strove to provide an environment which fostered a joy for living and learning. One of their mantras was "do it right, give it your best, and absolutely don't give up."

This included having a good attitude and staying focused. Roberta vividly remembered her mother's reminder as she escorted Bobbie to kindergarten class one morning: "Sit up front, listen to the teacher, and don't play with friends --- until recess."

Elementary school was her delight. Bobbie learned to read before she started school and her kindergarten teacher, Mrs. Beatty, nurtured her love for reading. She discovered she could travel and enjoy exciting adventures as the magic of words carried her imagination to unknown pleasures. In first grade, she read the most books in a reading contest and won a book entitled "Owls do the Darndest Things". As an adult, finding time to read a book was one of her greatest joys.

First grade also held special memories of her younger brother, who was her best friend. He came to her defense whenever he thought she was being bullied. The two of them shared everything; she was probably a teenager before she got a whole candy bar to herself, which was just fine with her.

Bobbie became a Brownie, her first introduction to Girl Scouts, and loved the outdoor activities and arts/crafts projects. She earned all her badges as she stayed focused and developed a good work ethic.

She was a daddy's girl who enjoyed sports, a walk through the woods, and being at his side as he worked on cars. Bobbie was daddy's little "tool-handler" --- when his big fingers couldn't grasp a screw, her small fingers eagerly reached in and got the job done.

Her family was close-knit and enjoyed spending time together. Long absences, necessitated by their military lifestyle, endeared the time spent with treasured extended family and close friends made along the way.

When Bobbie was in third grade, her dad was stationed in Hawaii for a second time. She was delighted to see the pink hospital where she'd been born and meet her godparents. Bobbie admired her godmother's compassionate heart and observed with interest as she and her husband opened their home and cared for mentally disabled men, most of whom had nowhere else to go.

Their next-door neighbor introduced Bobbie to a local version of sushi and Bobbie was hooked. She learned to hula dance, oil paint, swim, and developed a love for riding horses. Every Marine Base had horses and she learned western style riding, English jumping, and barrel racing. Always barefoot and outside, Bobbie's feet grew tough. She thought she wanted to be a beach bum. Walking the rough rock and dirt streets of Haiti was not even a remote thought in her head.

Her aunt and uncle, who lived in Michigan, always visited the family in each new place that became home. This act of love endeared them both to Bobbie and helped instill within her a strong sense of family.

When Bobbie was nine, the Vietnam War began and her dad was deployed 14 months. The rest of the family moved to Pasadena, CA, to live next door to the children's paternal grandmother, who doted on her granddaughter. Roberta remembered how they talked on the porch together and she treasured the many things she learned in her grandmother's kitchen, like how to poach an egg.

Both her grandmother and mother were immaculate in dress and style and the adult Roberta seemed to inherit the same flair. Roberta believed it's what's on the inside of a person that gives one worth, but she also thought the outside should honor God. Whether dressed in her Sunday best or walking the dusty streets of Haiti, she always managed to look beautiful.

In Pasadena, Bobbie and her brother had a special relationship with their cousin, John. The three became known as "The Three Musketeers." Frequent family cookouts found the children eating lots of beef, ice cream, and watermelon and exhausting themselves as they made up outdoor games to play while the adults visited and chatted.

Though these were pleasant days, the long family separations were taxing and plagued with spotty communication from her dad. Several months passed without a letter from Dad and then one day a shoebox-full arrived.

Re-entry of her dad into their homelife brought adjustments for everyone. Due to sheer fright, the dog urinated on the floor at the sight of this strange man; her dad periodically screamed out in the middle of the night; and her mom and dad had to re-learn parenting as a team.

After her dad's return from Viet Nam, the family moved to Quantico, VA, Bobbie's fifth year of grade school. Here, she slid down snowy hills, learned to play soccer, fell in love with turtles and fish, and found a new friend who also liked sports more than dolls.

Chapter 2
Middle School

The first half of sixth grade was spent in Jacksonville, FL, at the Holy Spirit Catholic School. From the very first day of school, her favorite teacher was Sister Noreen, who had "flaming red" hair and was a disciplinarian with a sense of humor. Roberta's heart was full of cherished memories as she recalled how proud she felt when the nun entrusted her with the ice cream money. It was under Sister Noreen's tutelage she learned to say "library", instead of "libary".

During the second half of Bobbie's sixth grade year, the family moved to Virginia Beach, VA, for two years. Her dad was on independent duty with the Navy on the USS Columbus in the Mediterranean and the Middle East. For a magical Christmas celebration, he flew his family to Barcelona and Madrid. It was in Madrid that Bobbie refused to eat a chicken that still had its feet.

While in Virginia Beach, Bobbie experienced her first spiritual awareness. She met Chaplain Dean Veltman, chaplain for the military base. He was a big, gentle man with a daughter, Kathy, who was also Bobbie's age. During Bible studies and on youth retreats, Bobbie began to understand the realness of God and how He desires a personal relationship with each of us.

Bobbie also discovered she enjoyed running track and was awarded the Top Star of the Presidential Fitness Award, revealing the athletic capabilities inherited from her parents.

Roberta

In middle school, Bobbie became a newspaper carrier and her brother often voluntarily awoke at 3:30 a.m. to help her. When she was old enough to drive, she worked at Burger King and her love for their hamburgers continued for years to come. Upon arriving from Haiti, our first stop was the nearest Burger King as we headed home to our house.

Though Bobbie's world was one filled with transitions, her mom and dad tried to make their family unit constant. They always ate their meals together, fostering a cohesiveness that held them tight during the storms in their lives. As a young boy, her dad had to work to help feed his family; food was scarce. As the head of his family, even in the early days of the Marine Corps when money was tight, he determined they would not skimp on food.

As their children grew, they took advantage of the travel perks that come with a military career. Much in the same way their family meals brought them together, these family trips strengthened their bonds. Their travelling was purposeful. Planning and research went on for weeks as they anticipated educational and fantastic vacations to places like the Smithsonian Institute, Amish communities, the Grand Canyon and various European cities. These were exciting times together as they learned about and experienced the many wonders outside their own world. They ate at fancy restaurants using their proper table manners taught at home.

Something else the children learned at home was never to use labels or slurs when speaking of, or to, people. She was taught the value of using people's names, never using terms such as "Black", "White", or "fat" to describe someone. Her parents knew it was just as important for Bobbie not to call people names as it was for the person on the receiving end.

Bobbie didn't realize her brown skin was different from white skin until she reached high school. Her parents modeled how to ignore slurs, innuendos, and outright rudeness while maintaining their dignity. Her mom emphasized the problem did not lie within Bobbie, but within those who spoke and behaved ignorantly --- lessons which served her well through the years.

Bobbie's dad made her feel safe and special as he shared his approach to life and his gentle, yet strong love for her, created a steadfast bond between them. He respected her as a person. For many years, it never occurred to her that she was not accepted by everyone, since she was so totally accepted by her dad.

Chapter 3
Realities of Life

During her high school and college years, Bobbie began to feel the injustices of bigotry in her life. She endured and triumphed over many demeaning encounters throughout her adult years.

She started high school in Peoria, IL, where they lived for three years while her dad was on an independent duty with the Marine Corps Reserves located at the Naval Reserve Training Center. They lived in one of 15 military houses located west of Peoria. Bobbie loved "living like a regular kid" as she attended public school and played basketball, ran track, and rode horses. She took a high school entrance exam and tested out of her entire freshman year. She well-remembered she wore a tan skirt and a shirt with a big red apple pin on her first day of high school.

Not only was she the only student of color in the high school, but the Ku Klux Klan (KKK) had regular meetings in the Naval Reserve Training Center. For their safety, her dad taught his wife and children how to shoot a gun. Because of these situations, Bobbie was not allowed to date until she was 17 years old.

But that didn't slow down Bobbie's social life; she thoroughly enjoyed her friends, both guys and gals. Her good buddies were Connie, Cary, and David --- they clowned around, enjoying good clean fun. One New Year's Eve, Bobbie and seven of her track-team friends piled into a yellow VW convertible and drove down the street as they beat old pots and pans, making a racket that could be heard for blocks.

During Bobbie's senior year, the family moved to Cherry Point, NC. Although she had enjoyed living off base for three years, her flexibility was evident in her ability to easily adjust to life on base once again. Cherry Point was also where she met her first real boyfriend, Ronnie. Claiming he wanted to marry Bobbie, he also wanted to date others after he dropped her at the door. Needless to say, that didn't work out.

George was her closest male friend from school and he comforted her when Bobbie and Ronnie broke up. They spent a lot of time together in the outdoors and shared a love of hot dogs with chili and onions. Bobbie was always attracted to intellectual men and George was a genius. He finally kissed her on her birthday and they became an item.

She tried out but did not make the cast of the play, "Camelot". Undeterred, she became a backstage worker and their crew won the State Championship that year.

Bobbie's relay team set a state record for the 880 and 440 relays. In academics, she excelled in accounting and was encouraged to attend Atlantic Christian College (ACC) in Wilson, NC, (later known as Barton College) for an accounting degree.

"Bobbie" turned into "Roberta" about this time in her life. During her freshman year at ACC, Roberta no longer attended church. Coming from a military background, she never experienced the segregation of blacks and whites she now faced within the southern churches. She attended devotionals on campus, however, and most importantly, she kept reading and searching the Scriptures for truth.

Because there were no black sororities or fraternities on this 94% white campus, Roberta started a black sorority in her sophomore year. Belatedly, the following year she received an invitation to join a white sorority.

A Clay Jar Too Soon Broken

Roberta was anonymously nominated for Homecoming Queen and she won! But her reign as queen was bittersweet. As George danced with her during the "Queen Dance", all but about 20 people left. She was not allowed to ride in the Wilson Christmas parade with the Homecoming Court because of threats of rock-throwing.

From Roberta's vantage point, she believed the college president to be a man of integrity and fairness, but he was fired at the end of the year. The following year, the new president refused to shake her hand when he met Roberta. Nonetheless, a door had been opened: three more black women became Homecoming Queens and, in her senior year, Roberta was elected President of the Student Council.

In six years, the relationship between George and Roberta never got serious enough for marriage. She finally told him she wanted to date other men. When George let her go, his friends assured him he had made a big mistake.

Chapter 4
Practicing for a Real Job

The year Roberta received her BS in Accounting from ACC, her father was sent to Japan. For the first time in her life, Roberta didn't relocate with her family and, instead, moved to Greensboro, NC. She worked for Bank America as an entry level financial analyst. Her first boss was a great teacher for his staff of 15, but in three months, she was transferred and found her new boss to be demanding and a micromanager. She resigned after a year, went back to Wilson and stayed with her brother.

Roberta needed time to figure out what career she wanted to pursue. She worked as a switchboard operator for the whole campus and signed a year's contract to be a Resident Assistant (RA) for one of the dorms of her alma mater. She met students who overcame huge physical and emotional problems to graduate. Some suffered from illnesses such as anorexia nervosa or Muscular Dystrophy and some had been rape victims. She was a help to them and they were an inspiration to her. Roberta would one day help poverty-stricken Haitians with their huge physical and emotional struggles. She was in God's training program, completely unaware.

Following her RA job at the dorm, Roberta worked for Merck, Sharp, and Dohme Pharmacy. Moving out of the dorm meant searching for an apartment. In the process, she called to inquire about an apartment and was warmly invited to look at the unit. As Roberta walked in the door, the receptionist glanced up and mouthed, "omg." After regaining her composure, she informed Roberta there were no available apartments.

At her new job, Roberta helped with label control and maintained accountability for bottles, caps, etc., at the pharmaceutical company. She learned about prescription medications and the different ways they affect people --- good information to have when living in Haiti, but she didn't know that yet.

Her next business venture was purchasing a small Sears franchise in Wilson. The state of North Carolina had a high illiteracy rate and Wilson, itself, was predominantly white and among the poorest towns in North Carolina. A depressed economy and a black proprietor made it especially challenging for Roberta to grow her new business. Her work ethic, determination, and skills not only enabled her to succeed, but also won Roberta an award after her first year. She had taken the highest percentage of sales and Sears, Roebuck, and Company honored her for "point of sale and maintenance". God was strengthening her to overcome bias and bigotry in Haiti, but she didn't know that yet.

One of Roberta's co-workers had a friend, Lydel, who invited her to worship at the Central Church of Christ. By this time, Roberta was earnestly seeking truth about God and His church. She bought a new Bible, took notes, and studied the passages the preacher used. She was thirsty for knowledge and spiritual guidance. Brother Pearsall, an elder there, knew more about the Bible than any person she had known, and he took great joy in teaching her. Roberta had never been around people who delved into the scriptures as deeply as did these folks. She and Brother Pearsall studied the Bible many hours together and in October 1992, Roberta was baptized.

After she managed the Sears store for five years, she sold it and took three months off to rest. During this time, she helped a brother in Christ tear off a roof to construct a second story on a building. She would be doing the very same thing in Haiti, but she didn't know that yet.

Roberta then managed a doctor's office for three years, still searching for what she couldn't name. Dr. Blair was taking over his father's practice and needed someone to computerize the records. The small staff consisted of the doctor, a nurse, a receptionist, and the office manager, Roberta. She assisted in non-management ways with the patients, typed charts, and helped with the medicines. All the while, she was accruing more skills to take to Haiti, but she didn't know that yet.

Though she enjoyed her work at the doctor's office, Roberta was yearning for something she couldn't quite envision. As a new Christian, she was hungry for the Word and eager to incorporate its truth into her life. The church nurtured Roberta's spiritual growth as they embraced and encouraged her.

Eighteen months after Roberta's baptism, Evelyn Boyd, 75 years old, visited her congregation and told of her recent mission trip to Cap Haitien, a coastal town in northern Haiti. Roberta said it was a "God moment": the theme of Evelyn's talk was "Lord, Send Me". As Evelyn told of her experiences, Roberta was inspired and endeavored to learn more about Haiti.

She knew Haiti shares the island of Hispaniola with the Dominican Republic in the Caribbean, about 600 miles southeast of Miami. What she didn't know was it is only about the size of Massachusetts with a population the size of Georgia.

Roberta could not grasp the depth of poverty in this country. More than half the people live below the poverty level without safe drinking water. Malnutrition is rampant. Education is available only for those able to pay for tuition, books, and uniforms.

Roberta

She also discovered a wide practice of a different kind of child abuse little known to those of us living in America. Restaveks are destitute children forced into in a modern-day kind of slavery, oftentimes cooking food he will not eat and washing clothes she will not wear. They are forced to sleep on the floor or ground and most are physically and/or sexually abused. Approximately 1 in 15 Haitian children are restaveks such as these.

In a few days after Evelyn's talk, Roberta learned that Polly and Charlie were to lead a mission team to Cap Haitien. These friends from sister congregations were leaving in two weeks. One of the original team members cancelled at the last moment and Roberta was invited to take her place. She would need $1500, a passport, and the required vaccines in just eight days.

She had no passport, nor did she have $1500. It was truly amazing when $1700 was raised in just two days by Christians and friends. Equally astonishing, her passport arrived four days after she applied --- an exceptional turnaround as compared to the usual six-week wait period at that time. Roberta's employer, Dr. Blair, provided the vaccines at no cost. Eight days later, she was in Haiti.

Roberta shared this story with me several times, always as awed and animated as when first she told me. Looking back at the incredible ease with which she had gotten to Haiti, she could see the thread of God's plan woven through the whole experience. She was excited and amazed at how ably and personally God was working in her life.

Before her departure, Roberta had episodes of shortness of breath. The doctor said these were panic attacks. Roberta remembered the scripture from II Timothy 1:7, "For God has not given us a spirit of timidity, but of power and love and discipline." As Roberta owned this truth, she no longer panicked, but instead felt empowered.

Roberta and Evelyn were roommates on that trip and Roberta had to trot to keep up with her, impressed by the older woman's spirit and vigor. During their week together, Evelyn shared her amazing story with Roberta. In her early 60's and newly widowed, she first traveled to Haiti about ten years before. Because Evelyn had dared to say "yes" to God, a school of preaching, a senior citizens' home, schools, and medical clinics have all been established in rural northern Haiti.

During President Aristide's embargo on Haiti around 1993, there were no imports arriving and most Haitians were starving. This determined older woman flew into the Dominican Republic, was smuggled into Haiti using a small fishing boat, and walked two hours through marsh as she carried funds to hungry Christians. She broke an arm on this adventure, went home, and came back again. Even lung cancer didn't stop her for many years. Her selfless dedication and tenacity were unmatched in Roberta's eyes, setting an example of faith and servitude which bolstered Roberta for years to come.

Haiti captured Roberta's heart. Although this was her first visit, Roberta felt she had come home. Her heart ached over the poverty and devastation which surrounded her. One afternoon a little girl sat beside her looking thin, dirty, and hungry. Roberta offered the child a package of peanut butter crackers. The little girl nibbled on one of them and put the rest in her pocket. Through a translator, Roberta learned the rest of the crackers were for her brothers and sisters at home. This little girl's selflessness inspired Roberta to want to do more. The memory remained close to her heart always.

Roberta returned home with a restless heart which now belonged to Haiti and she believed she had found her purpose in this world. She had no plans of her own but was willing to trust God's plan for her: "You will make known to me the path of life; in Your presence is fullness of joy; in Your right hand there are pleasures forever." Psalm 16:11

Roberta

PART II
Headed Home

"I will lift up my eyes to the hills; from where shall my help come? My help comes from the Lord, who made heaven and earth. He will not allow your foot to slip; He who keeps you will not slumber."

Psalm 121:1-3

Chapter 5
Ice Cream and Walks on the Beach

Four days after Roberta returned home from Haiti, a young Haitian came to visit her congregation. He found his way to the United States under the guidance of Jesse Robertson. Jesse, a college student at Freed Hardeman University in Henderson, TN, met this man on a mission trip to Haiti. Jesse and fellow teammate, Scott Miskelly, helped him enroll into Freed-Hardeman.

After graduating, he traveled to North Carolina to raise funds to support his preaching ministry upon his return to Haiti. He arrived on a Thursday and that evening he and Roberta were introduced at the church cook-out. He was enthusiastic and felt compelled to spread the Good News in Haiti. Conversation came easily for the young people as he shared his story and she eagerly told him of the passion for Haitian children growing within her heart.

The next three days were spent walking on the beach, eating ice cream, and talking non-stop about Haiti. He mowed her lawn, washed her car, shared lunch at her kitchen table, and played with Roberta's beloved Rottweiler dog, Sheba.

At the end of his visit to Wilson, Roberta was amazed when he asked her to marry him. Her response was, "You're crazy!" He told Roberta he'd call in two weeks for her answer and left for Amory, MS, the location of his supporting congregation. Two weeks later, the call came. He asked if she was praying for guidance about marrying him. Roberta tried to make him understand she hardly knew him; talk of marriage was premature. He was soon on a quest for her to get to know him, talking for hours over the next days and weeks while he traveled and raised support money.

This young man was pulling her in a different direction than most of the people surrounding Roberta. She knew in her heart she had to go back to Haiti. She tried to share with friends and family the battle taking place within her mind and heart. American wealth and the lifestyle it afforded conflicted with the extreme poverty she witnessed in Haiti. Why did she buy yet another pair of shoes to go with her other 15 pairs when there was an urgent need to find food for a starving child? Why did she spend so much on entertainment and pleasure when the same money could give a child a safe place to live? For the first time in her life, she was asking herself hard questions from which she could not run.

Feeling the burden of suffering children was not new to Roberta. During her high school and college years, she financially supported a child in another third world country, seeing the child through to high school graduation. But now, as an adult, she could give more than financially --- she could use her very life to ease the burden of struggling children. What was hindering her?

These were the kind of questions that made friends feel uncomfortable and at a loss to help in her decision-making. They could not understand this overwhelming, intense need to minister in a third world country. Roberta said they seemed almost fearful they, too, might catch whatever she had.

She was confounded and frustrated. This young preacher's voice was the only one which seemed to make sense.

As they broached the subject of marriage, he tried to create a mental image of possible circumstances in which they might find themselves while living in Haiti --- maybe in a mud hut without electricity or perhaps on a mountain. The one thing he did know was that he needed her to help him spread the Gospel to the people of Haiti.

As Roberta listened to his need and desire to take the Gospel to Haiti and how he needed her by his side to help him, she kept thinking about her own journey in recent years. Roberta couldn't deny God's divine guidance in her life --- her spiritual journey to faith, the skills she learned through the years, provision of a passport and money for that first trip to Cap Haitien in just eight days' time, meeting Evelyn Boyd, and then the timely arrival of a young Haitian preacher. In early August, she accepted his proposal.

The Amory Church of Christ in Mississippi was overseeing this young man's plan to raise funds and return to Haiti. The elders invited Roberta for a visit and sent her a ticket. She thought they were talking about a plane ticket. Roberta also didn't know they thought she was white and were concerned the bi-racial marriage would present even more obstacles in a third world setting. She headed to Amory.

A road-weary Roberta arrived at the bus stop at 4:00 a.m. and was lovingly met by her fiancée and warmly welcomed by Paul and Jean Dickerson, an elder and his wife in the Amory church. Paul talked to her like a daughter, trying to bring realism to a life as a missionary. He said, "It will take 15 to 20 years of hard work to establish a church of Christ." As it turned out, 20 years was all Roberta had to give.

Roberta stayed in Amory for an enjoyable week filled with conversation of the couple's upcoming plans, enjoying ice cream and walks along the Dickerson's country driveway. She was impressed with her new fiancée's pristine appearance and how well he presented himself. It became evident to Roberta that this man loved his people and wanted only to preach and spread the Word.

The two of them studied the scriptures and prayed a lot during their short time together. He could speak Spanish and he quoted chapters of scriptures in Creole, French, and English. As you may remember, Roberta was attracted to intellectual men and this man's intellect and education surpassed any she had known.

Her parents, on the other hand, were seriously unimpressed with this potential son-in-law. When Roberta brought him home, her mother thought him lazy with an attitude of entitlement. Compounding their feelings about this man, they had serious objections to Roberta even being a missionary in Haiti. A deep chasm was created between parents and daughter, one that never really went away. Each held their ground strongly in the conflict. Her parents did not speak to her for three years.

On August 19, 1995, Roberta married. Oh, how she anticipated returning home to a place she hardly knew but had captured her heart so completely. Along with the excitement came the laborious task of deciding what possessions they could take across the ocean. Early on, as the two young people began negotiating, Roberta's one request had been to take her dog. Her fiancée responded, "Sure, Honey." However, as they loaded the car just three hours before heading back to Amory, he abruptly changed his mind; it was Haiti (him) or the dog. Roberta was heart-broken and bewildered.

They drove to Amory to say goodbye and the church hosted a big send-off party with gifts and a money tree to help with moving expenses. Upon being asked what the couple needed to take with them, the groom assured the church all he needed were his books. The elders asked, "What about your wife's things?" Another jolt.

Chapter 6
Unexpected Surprises of the Fearful Type

Afraid of flying, her new husband trembled during the entire flight and revealed to Roberta there were snipers waiting to kill him. He believed these men were jealous of his education and feared he would try to displace a favored local preacher. Because he had American connections, they saw him as powerful, rich, and a serious threat to their livelihood.

Their arrival in Port-au-Prince was chaotic, heightening the trepidation Roberta was feeling since talk of an assassination had first arisen. Mass confusion reigned. The unbearable heat in the tiny, overcrowded, non-air-conditioned airport was not only suffocating, but reeked with body odor.

Outside was no better. Because President Aristide's embargo prevented help from other countries, Haiti was in a mess: stench filled the air from random piles of garbage; black pigs rooted in the garbage and swam in mudholes; and smelly, rotting foodstuff and trash filled the opened concrete ditches alongside the road. The streets themselves held rubbish and were lined with vendors desperately trying to sell mangos, souvenirs, packets of water, sugar cane, etc. The couple left the airport amidst starving people who mobbed them, over-zealously trying to sell their goods.

Roberta

Food is Scarce Even for Pigs

Free of the airport, the confused couple had no idea where they would stay the night. The Holiday Inn was full, so they went to the Oloffson Hotel and slept fitfully. They later learned it was a voodoo hotel and their unease was for good reason --- voodoo ceremonies were held there weekly, as they do even in 2019.

Fortunately, a room in the Holiday Inn was available the following day and they spent their first day sleeping from exhaustion. "Certified" restaurants for Americans were expensive and it was out of the question for them to eat all their meals there. The couple ate once a day at the hotel restaurant and then ate bread and bananas. Concerned about contamination, Roberta did not drink the water.

The checks in their pockets were of no help, since checks were required to be in the bank 45 days before withdrawal, causing a financial hardship.

As the days went by, Roberta began adding rice, beans, and a little chicken into her diet (cooked by street vendors or her husband's family). She began feeling unwell with nausea and vomiting. Americans must build a resistance to food bacteria that Haitians ingest daily. With a lack of refrigeration and different standards of food preparation and storage, Haitians can tolerate foods that otherwise cause food poisoning in Americans. To compound her sick stomach, the stench of dead bodies in the park across from their hotel was unbearable.

There was little diesel fuel available in the country, leaving few tap-taps available for transportation. A tap-tap is a small pick-up truck with benches in the back and a topper, used as a taxi service.

TapTap, Alex May, and Roberta

Exhausted from walking in the extreme heat and on dusty roads, they decided to rent a car for a few days. Roberta quickly learned she would be the designated driver since her new husband had never driven. Driving the narrow, overcrowded streets filled with potholes is no easy feat, even for the experienced. There are precious few red lights and drivers can drive on any part of the road they so choose.

The day they left the Holiday Inn and moved in with her husband's aunt, Roberta retrieved the car while he took care of the luggage and checked them out. Unfamiliar with the unmarked streets and the confusion of many one-way streets, she ended up going in circles. When she finally found her way back to the hotel 2 ½ hours later, he was panicked, yelling at the hotel manager to find his wife. His relief was evident as he treated Roberta with gentleness, thankful she was safe.

They moved into his aunt's tiny house where there were many other family members living, none of whom spoke English. She was put in a chair with no introductions while the relatives stared unashamedly. No one made attempts to communicate with Roberta, leaving her feeling isolated and a spectacle.

Determinedly, however, she slowly learned the ways and customs of the Haitian people, including the important task of drawing water from a well. Mastering the water bucket and the well became a personal goal for Roberta. She guided the bucket gently and smoothly as it went down the side of the well and then, with a controlled quick movement, enabled the bucket to gently dip into the water without disturbing the silt. She pulled it up while balancing atop a tire, with one foot on either side. Many buckets of murky water were drawn until she finally succeeded. Accomplishing this small feat gave her a sense of not only victory but hope that she could succeed in the many challenges she knew faced her.

It was a bright spot in Roberta's life when her mother-in-law visited for several weeks. For Roberta's first Haitian cuisine lesson, his mother taught her to cook kalalou and bef (okra and beef). This, too, gave Roberta a sense of accomplishment and encouraged her determination to conquer the feelings of inadequacy that plagued her.

Having returned the rental car, the pair walked many miles each day, finding people with whom to share the Gospel. Typically, her preacher-husband began talking on the street and soon 20 to 50 people would gather around. This worked for a while, but a car was needed to reach even more people. Diesel fuel was becoming more available, though still costly.

A Clay Jar Too Soon Broken

The church in Amory said they would provide money for the couple to purchase a vehicle --- not an easy task when you live in Haiti.

Her brother-in-law, a bank manager, lived in a coastal town with a port, south of Port au Prince. Because they thought he could expedite delivery of a car, the couple journeyed down to visit. They rode in a tap-tap overcrowded with people and live chickens. The trip took four hours, one way. At one point, the man next to her laid his head on Roberta's lap. Her American need for personal space was violated and she "totally freaked out". Her husband asked the man to move his head, which he did. They made the round-trip journey in one day, thoroughly exhausted and covered with dust and grime when they finally arrived back at his aunt's house.

As they got further into the process of trying to bring a US vehicle into Haiti, Roberta began to understand that "timetables" and "Haiti" are incompatible. Rarely did the company have their paperwork ready for an appointment, nor did the couple have all their paperwork in place, since they had not been told what was needed.

During this time period, the newlyweds moved from his aunt's house into a motel/apartment in Petionville, a suburb east of Port-au-Prince in the hills. It was one large room with a bed, refrigerator, stove, and bath. They thoroughly enjoyed having their own space. The Caribbean grocery store was not far away and Roberta enjoyed her daily walk to purchase whatever food they needed and could afford. One day she saw a little bit of home laying there on a shelf --- a Snickers candy bar! Silently she did a little dance and hurried out of the store in great anticipation. Tearing it open, she found the candy covered with bugs. As she dealt with the disappointment, she experienced the reality of the embargo: all supplies were low, and none were fresh.

It took five brutal trips south to complete the forms allowing them to ship a vehicle to Haiti. On one of the journeys, they spent the night with Roberta's brother-in-law and his family because numerous manifestations made it unsafe to travel after dark. Manifestations are demonstrations in the streets, majorly against the government, with intentional roadblocks, tire burnings, rock-throwing, or all three --- always dangerous.

Though the house was tiny, it was tidy and clean sheets were on the bed. Without windows in the house, the heat was stifling. Eight people lived there. The only bed was given to the newlyweds.

Located in the countryside, nighttime was so black Roberta couldn't see her hand in front of her face. Her sense of hearing, however, was just fine as she lay sweating on her pillow, listening to the buzzing of mosquitoes around her head. During the night, something moved in their bed and Roberta felt a furry creature brush her. The family laughed when she reported it the next morning, but no one bothered to look for it.

Anyone who has the faith and determination to live in a third world country with an unstable government, kidnapping threats, and machetes must be a tough and courageous person. To learn of her fear of rats and spiders --- well, it just made me giggle.

Still cautious about Haitian-cooked food, breakfast for Roberta the next morning was bread and a warm Coke. As they headed back to Petionville, the country remained in disarray with tire burnings and loud, angry gatherings, making travel difficult. The trip took a grueling 12 hours, the last four spent walking up the mountain in the dark. Totally exhausted upon arriving home, they feasted on peanut butter sandwiches and warm Cokes, then collapsed onto their bed.

Her husband's brother got a deal for the car to arrive in his port instead of the port at Port-au-Prince. The Amory elders had growing concerns about this arrangement for several reasons: they didn't know the brother-in-law, they didn't have a solid understanding of the Haitian government's regulations concerning shipping a vehicle into Haiti, and lastly, a lot of money was involved. The deal with the brother was not pursued and Roberta went car-shopping in Miami instead, with instructions to ship the vehicle to the bigger city of Port-au-Prince.

Roberta arrived in Miami on a Wednesday evening, rented a car, bought a newspaper, and found two possible vehicles. No one picked up on the first number dialed, but the second number was answered and she was quoted a price. She called the church in Amory and the response was, "Where do we send the funds?" They trusted Roberta completely.

At 6:00 the next morning, map in hand, she managed to find the address. Roberta looked under the hood, examined the transmission, belts, and checked the oil. Working on cars with Daddy had paid off. The owner was impressed and complimented her knowledge of cars.

Money was transferred, the title was changed, and the truck was on the dock by 2:00 p.m. --- all pertinent papers registered. In less than 36 hours in an unfamiliar city and no GPS, she had found a car, purchased it, arranged for shipping, and was on the next flight back to Haiti. That black Nissan truck was seen being driven on the streets of Haiti just four years ago, 20 years later. Such longevity is virtually unheard of in Haiti, whose roads are filled with cavernous potholes and stones.

Feeling happy with her mission well-accomplished, Roberta returned home. She had experienced for two weeks the harsh, brutal life Haiti promised her and, yet, amazingly it never crossed her mind not to go back.

Chapter 7
Struggling with Loneliness

Even after moving into their own apartment, her husband continued to take Roberta back to his aunt's house and left her alone for long periods of time while he went to preach and teach. Roberta's inability to communicate with his relatives felt more oppressive as time moved on. Unable to endure it any longer, one day she walked the five miles back to the apartment, uphill most of the way. Roberta's loneliness grew worse. Initially, seeing other missionaries in the grocery store excited her and was a day-brightener, until repeatedly they just walked away without exchanging pleasantries. The only reason she could discern for their coldness was race --- they were white and she was black.

There were times when the couple was cooped up inside the apartment for a day or two, due to the numerous holidays in which the city closed its doors of businesses or demonstrations made it too dangerous to be on the streets. Roberta enjoyed her husband's cooking lessons during these long days and the in-depth Bible studies they shared. She wanted to be a good preacher's wife and, as she read the Bible and his many commentaries, her wisdom and knowledge grew. Haiti's climate is hot and living areas are small with few windows and fans. To be able to concentrate for hours, as they dug deeply into the Scriptures, had to have been a true test of mind over body.

Roberta

A month after moving into their new apartment, Roberta became plagued by fevers. There were no doctors, so she used her first-aid kit to treat herself. For days, none of the usual remedies abated the nausea, vomiting, and fevers caused from ingesting contaminated food and water. Her body was struggling to fight. At the height of her illness, her husband stayed up all night fanning her. Finally, the symptoms abated as the tainted food left her body. She lost 60 pounds in the first six months in her new country. Over time, Roberta learned better how to eat and drink safely and her health stabilized.

A call home for comfort and encouragement was not an option. Not only was it expensive, but her parents were still bitterly disappointed about her marriage and her move to Haiti.

When all that was familiar and comforting to Roberta was an ocean away and the language barrier hindered friendships in Haiti, she relied heavily on her Lord for comfort and strength. She accompanied her husband whenever possible as he went out and preached. As she witnessed the joy on the faces of those responding to the Good News, her own desire to teach was kindled and intensified, bringing encouragement in her loneliness. Roberta knew she wanted to teach the women in their own language.

Initially, the newlyweds found it difficult to find a church with whom to worship and they discovered ugly truths about corruption in the church and the coldness of Christians. In Port-au-Prince, they had their first encounter in preacher-scamming. They showed up ten minutes early and the door was locked. At 9:00, the door was opened. By 9:45, there were seven or eight people. At 10:30, a big car arrived with the preacher and his wife. Roberta said he didn't preach the Gospel and his message was angrily presented in French, not understood by the average Haitian. He told Roberta he could help her get her driver's license and cash their checks for them with 20% going into his pocket. This was the first of many such disappointments she and her husband would face in their ministry.

As they worshipped with yet another congregation, Roberta felt like they were in a satanic place. It was a similar feeling to the one they experienced at the Oloffson Hotel their first night in Port-au-Prince. She said the feeling was hard to describe: there was a restlessness she felt in the presence of some unknown evil and there was a strong urge to get out of the building. They kept looking.

Periodically, they worshipped with an average-sized congregation of 50-100 people. One Sunday morning the twosome visited unannounced and found hundreds of people at worship. They learned that Haitian people had been paid to come and hear the American preachers so there would be a "good showing", not an uncommon practice they later learned.

Having a large crowd at worship implied a growing, healthy church, which meant more American dollars willingly invested in the ministry. Local preachers who were guilty of this practice perceived Roberta and her husband as threats to their jobs, afraid they would report the activity to American elders. Their relationships became strained.

The church in Amory continued to be supportive and wrote out a plan for their future: now that the car had been purchased, they would purchase property, build their house, build the church building, and, finally, purchase a second vehicle. At one point, two of the Amory elders traveled to Haiti with money to purchase land and a building, but Roberta's husband told them it was "too soon". This turned out to be one of the wiser decisions he made.

The couple needed time to figure out together the tough issue of finances. As a preacher who watched over many needy people, he tended to be overly generous when people sought him out for help with food, rent, or medicine. Oftentimes this meant using budgeted monies as he tried to satisfy unending needs of the people. Roberta tried to help him see a balance. Her philosophy was, "You don't start something with a hundred people that you can't do for a thousand." In other words, she thought it unwise to help people in ways that could not be continued as the numbers grew. People would not understand why you once helped them and now you won't.

They continued to walk everywhere, preaching, teaching, and visiting other congregations. When the Nissan arrived, her brother-in-law got the customs' cost down to a reasonable tax. Taxes and fees (such as custom fees paid when bringing certain items into a foreign country) are often negotiable and exploited in Haiti. After receiving their car, preacher and wife soon reached more people in more towns. They traveled over the rocky, bumpy, narrow roads to little towns and villages, preaching the Word. He took out his Bible, as was usual for him, and began to teach one person on the street. As always, by the time he finished, a large crowd had gathered. People were hungry for truth and this man had the knowledge and a charismatic way of sharing God's Word.

Chapter 8
Buying a House

For several months, her husband preached Monday through Friday and took Saturday off. Christ's message spread throughout the Port-au-Prince area, but without a place for people to come to worship, there was no stability. The two sought a place to settle down to grow a church.

In early 1996, they met an ex-communicated Catholic priest who invited the couple to come to Santo for a visit. Finding no one home upon arriving, they decided to explore the small community and fell in love with Santo, located on the northeast side of Port-au-Prince.

Though most dwellings were one-room mud houses, they found a concrete house with a large dining/living room. They began filling out the rental agreement but had to leave before finishing, due to a Bible study appointment. As was often the case, the preacher talked too long and they found the house rented to someone else upon their return.

Disappointed, they kept looking and praying. To their surprise, two weeks later the owner met them on the street with news the other deal had fallen through; the house was again available. Roberta was elated to have her own space where she could breathe freely and own cows, goats, and chickens. But most of all, she was excited to offer a safe and welcoming place for people to come and worship --- people eager to hear the Word. Having her own space also rescued Roberta from the peering eyes and scrutiny of her husband's family and friends who still saw her as an oddity and treated her as such. As they moved into the house, her husband mentioned he was going to hire a cook for her. Roberta was leery since the language barrier made for difficult communication.

With a permanent place to worship and daily teaching and invitations by the young couple, the number of people coming to worship increased dramatically. The congregation soon grew from 70 to 100 people. Roberta and her husband arose at 5:30 in the morning and worked until 9:00 at night. They set up a first-aid station to take care of medical needs such as delivery of babies, machete cuts, and burns. They gave out food, counseled married couples, and conducted innumerable Bible studies.

Providing chairs for all who came to worship was a challenge. They traveled as far as Miragoane, sometimes returning empty-handed but other times with 15 or so. Eventually, the couple owned 300 chairs. Followers of Jesus were being baptized every Sunday.

Roberta believed her husband to be an effective preacher, excelling in his Bible knowledge and having an affable personality. People of all social levels responded to the message eagerly because he knew how to bring the Bible to a level anyone could understand. He began where they were, both spiritually and physically. He held up a Bible in the streets and asked, "What does this mean?" He spoke to his audience about God's plan for His people, Jesus the Christ, teaching Genesis through Revelation.

He played soccer, cards, and dominoes and even playfully put girls' headbands in his hair as he tried to relate to people of all ages and genders. He was like a pied piper. While women washed clothes in the river, they told him they had no time to listen. He just rolled up his sleeves and started washing clothes. They laughed, gave him 15 minutes and were at worship the following Sunday morning.

The couple strove to be the light in their community as they lived and worked among their neighbors and as they moved around the city. Roberta recalled riding a tap-tap as a woman, with her baby, tried to board. The driver moved before she was completely on board and she was dragged. The young couple helped get the driver's attention and assisted her onto the tap-tap. When the two women's paths crossed again seven or eight years later, the woman remembered Roberta.

After a year and a half, the elders called their young missionary back to the States. They had initially found it hard to believe the reports of all the baptisms. Upon hearing how many hours a day the couple worked, going out amongst the people and becoming a part of their lives, the elders became convinced God was blessing the work and, indeed, remarkable things were taking place in Santo, Haiti.

Though they now had a car, the pair continued to spend part of their time walking through Santo, determined not to become known as "the preacher with the car". They wanted very much for the emphasis to be on the message, not the messengers. Without the trapping of the car there was one less obstacle to separate them from the people.

But that also became problematic. Walking caused a scandal. In Haitian culture, the preacher does not walk and most certainly not his American wife, who they perceived to be of noble birth. Preachers in Haiti are often automatically given an unearned status of privilege and are expected to ride in cars, not walk around like commoners. The couple was trying to set Christ's example of selfless, compassionate love --- no one is better than another. "Do nothing out of selfish ambition or vain conceit. Rather, in humility value others above yourselves" (Philippians 2:3).

As she accompanied her husband in his daily teaching, Roberta still struggled with Creole, the common language of Haiti. Creole comes from a blend of French, African languages, and Spanish. France conquered Haiti and enslaved the native people, adding them to the slaves they brought from Africa. The Spanish influence came through sharing the island with the Dominican Republic. Though most common people speak Creole, the elite (Bourgeoisie) speak French. Most schools in Haiti teach in French, though the students and even some of the teachers, themselves, don't understand French.

Roberta had a difficult time learning Creole, picking up bits and pieces during her everyday routine. But she was convicted the children needed a Bible class of their own and she courageously decided to teach them on Sunday mornings. Unfortunately, there were no Creole translation books at that time and it took Roberta all week to prepare her class. She translated her lesson into Creole and then practiced speaking it, so the children could understand her. In addition to the lesson, she also needed to help them learn to sit still during the class and not wander off to play or take care of personal needs at a nearby tree.

As the weeks went by, Roberta noticed a new phenomenon evolving. People were arriving 30 minutes early for class and worship, unheard of in the Haitian culture. When the gate to their property was opened at 9:30 a.m., half the church was present and waiting. As had been their experience since their arrival, God's Word was received with joy and enthusiasm. The big challenge ahead was to help the people free themselves of voodoo influence.

The new congregation was blooming, but thorns of discontent and mistrust were present as well, especially in Roberta's home. The topic of hiring a cook for Roberta arose sharply again. Her husband insisted it was the Haitian way and wanted to hire Fabienne, a cousin of a friend. Roberta felt it unwise because the woman didn't speak English nor was Roberta proficient in Creole. She believed miscommunication was far more harmful than no communication. But, as in so many other ways, Roberta's voice fell on deaf ears in the conflict of cultures.

Fabienne was hired and life became more complicated. Roberta's Christian background and Fabienne's Haitian culture clashed with one another. A residual effect of Haiti's slave era is the "slave mentality", as Roberta expressed it. They expect to be used by each other, by their employers, or any person they perceive as "higher" than themselves. Exploitation is a way of life for them. People who love, forgive, and respect one another are viewed as "crazy"; their kindness is seen as a ploy.

As an employee, Fabienne believed she had manipulated and taken advantage of Roberta when her misdeeds and attitudes were not met with railings and anger. She viewed Roberta's acts of kindness, forgiveness, and respect as inappropriate behavior for a respectable boss; she mistook kindness for weakness and forgiveness for gullibility. Roberta considered Fabienne a companion and thought they had a close relationship. It soon became evident that it was a misplaced trust on Roberta's part. Fabienne's loyalty belonged to the preacher.

As time went by, Roberta grew steadily weaker and suffered with a never-ending queasy stomach. A friend observed what was happening and suggested that Roberta was slowly being poisoned by Fabienne, who might be adding plant poison to Roberta's food and placing voodoo curses on her. After the cook was fired, Roberta got better.

Thankful she was no longer in harm's way, Roberta felt better and was more energized to focus again on the church and her community. As Americans responded to her plea for financial help, monies were sent for medical supplies and to send some of the children to school. Roberta was given the title of "Doctor" and she was reminded of well-spent time in Dr. Blair's office several years earlier, grateful for the ways in which God helped prepare her. In reality, there is no way of arriving in Haiti fully prepared --- you just hold on to God's hand and dive in.

Roberta saw the need for good nutrition, if the children were to have any success as students. Though she had no finances, she dreamt of a Nutrition Center to serve the students breakfast and lunch. Nine-year-old Marchodson, a little neighbor boy, would come to her yard early in the morning before school and awakened Roberta as he threw rocks at the mango trees to bring down enough fruit to share with the other children. Families often had no food but drank sugar water and ate clay "biscuits" (made from dirt, sugar, oil, and water) to abate the deep hunger pangs. The poverty level was such that families were starving, especially the babies and small children.

Osnel and Roberta

Osnel was the very first child Roberta helped in Haiti. His mother died giving him birth and he was handed around in the family. When Roberta first saw him in 1996, he wore grey cut-off sweatpants, a ragged red-and-blue girl's blouse, and no shoes. He slept and worked in their yard, picking up rocks, sticks, and trash. Osnel very much wanted to learn to read and write, so Roberta tutored him for a year and held his hand to form letters on his paper. He was number one in his class for his first three years of school. In later years, she broke out in a big grin whenever she saw him walk through her gate.

As she helped Osnel, it whetted Roberta's appetite to do more for the children. Roberta asked friends in the States for money to keep the Nutrition Center children in school and feed them two meals each day. Whenever possible, Roberta gave from her own pocket if funds didn't stretch. They soon were feeding 120 children daily in the newly formed Nutrition Center.

Three more children joined Osnel in the preacher's yard. Five-year-old David ate regularly at the Nutrition Center. After his mother's death, David asked Roberta if he could take food to his brother, Sylvio, whom David had been protecting and helping, as best he could. Surprised he had never mentioned a brother, she accompanied David home and met Sylvio.

What she discovered horrified her. Sylvio lay on a flat cardboard box under a tree, unbathed and naked. At one time, the boys lived in a house made of hay, which collapsed on Sylvio when the rotting support sticks collapsed. There was no electricity or indoor plumbing and water was carried up from the creek.

Sylvio's family feared him because they did not know what was wrong. One of his saddest memories was lying under a tree, watching as his grave was dug and his coffin built; they expected him to die at any moment.

At age twelve, Sylvio was the size of a seven-year-old. His body was covered with sores, his eyes were jaundiced, and his urine was the color of Coca-Cola. Roberta took the young boy to the doctor, a first for Sylvio, and discovered he had sickle-cell anemia, a life-threatening blood condition if left untreated. The two youngsters came to live in the preacher's yard.

When he was about 19 years of age, Sylvio wrote a letter to a friend which included this excerpt:

Roberta

"God had sent Roberta and her husband to Santo to start preaching the Gospel, plant a congregation, and a nutrition center. My little brother, David was already in the center and going to church at the congregation there. He asked Roberta if I could come and eat every day and Roberta allowed me to come. I got to eat two big meals a day. Roberta even paid for me to go to school. I was so happy to start a new life. I had medicines and was feeling better. My mother died in 1998 and Roberta took me and my brother David and raised us as her own. I have been with her ever since. God has given me a new family. I have fourteen brothers and sisters. I am thankful for the grace and blessings the Lord has bestowed on me.

"I want to be a doctor when I finish my undergraduate school. Every day I wake up and thank God for another day of life. I don't know what happened to that coffin, but God's plans are bigger than any of us can even think."

In April of 2006, Sylvio was able to travel to the States and receive medical treatment for the quarter-size hole in the top of his foot. At the writing of this book, he is 31 years old and still struggles with persistent sores that won't heal. He is married, has a toddler, and is working for an orphanage in Haiti, "Hope for Haiti's Children". He reports his wife just graduated from high school.

David and Sylvio arrived in 1996, a year after the newlyweds moved to Haiti. A few days later, a third young man arrived, Widlord Thomas. His dad brought the 12-year-old to Roberta's house for the weekend and never returned for him.

Thomas, the oldest and only son of five children, lived with his family in a small two-room house made of sticks and mud. The children slept on the floor while the parents slept in the only bed. There was no running water, electricity, or inside toilets. Thomas was sent two or three times a day for water.

He went often because he could only carry two gallons of water at a time on the hour-long trip.

There was never enough food. Many days they had only one meal; other days they went without completely. Out of desperation, his mother sometimes bought food on credit; when collection time rolled around, she scrambled to pay her debts. After Roberta opened her Nutrition Center, Thomas came and ate and ate because he was so hungry.

On occasion, Thomas' mother found money to send him to school, but many times he was sent home due to late school payments. Since students were required to wear uniforms, Thomas learned to pack a t-shirt in his backpack for such days, so no one knew he was a student "going home in disgrace".

His little body was very tall and thin and the deep voice coming forth from his mouth was a surprise. His clothes were habitually too little. He never had but one pair of shoes at a time, wearing them until they could no longer be sewn up or re-glued, although his feet had outgrown them. After Thomas moved in, Roberta noticed he was walking in an unusual way and questioned him. She went straight away and bought him a pair of shoes. He didn't want to tell her the new shoes were also too small because he was fearful he would have to do without --- too small was better than none. But Roberta was watchful and found him the correct size. Thomas, about 6'2", has never forgotten the sheer joy of walking without pain and still appreciates a good-fitting pair of shoes.

In a letter Thomas wrote to a friend years ago, he spoke of his goals to finish high school and attend college to study Bible and Business at Freed-Hardeman University in Henderson, TN.

He expressed thankfulness to Roberta and his Christian brothers and sisters in the States who helped her, because he was no longer sleeping on the floor. When Sonlight received more visitors than they had beds, it was a pleasure for him to give up his bed for his brethren. Thomas also said, "I have food to eat and medicine when I am sick. I have clothes and shoes that fit. The most important thing I have is Christ in my life. My sisters and birth parents still live in the mud house and there are many other kids that are living the way that I lived. I hope someday to help other children that are suffering like I did." Thomas believes the trials he experienced as a child helped deepen his faith in Jesus.

With generous help from a friend, Sherry Brooks, Thomas was able to get to the States, and receive his Graduation Equivalency Diploma (GED). Many gracious people in the church forged a path for Thomas, now known as Widlord, to graduate from Freed-Hardeman University with honors in December 2014.

Thomas

He met Karen Day and married her in October 2015. Currently the couple live in Ft. Worth, TX, where Widlord, now 33 years old, preaches for a small church in Paris, TX, and drives an Amazon delivery truck. He and Karen are the proud parents of two boys: David, named after Widlord's father and Robert, named after Widlord's grandfather. Robert is called Bobbie in memory of Roberta.

Chapter 9
Deceit, Distrust, and Destruction

In three years, the church grew to 450 members, 200 of whom were children, and they met in the yard of the young couple. Many of those children are still faithful today. People were hungry for the truth. The rich began sitting by the poor, closing cultural gaps.

When children are fed and educated, parents feel hope, perhaps for the first time. Jesus' light is displacing the darkness in their lives. In steps Satan. Satan is the great destroyer and destroy he did.

For most of the first three years, things were good in the young marriage. At one point, Roberta's husband told the elders he had the wife described in Proverbs 31. But in that third year, he began talking and acting strangely. At first Roberta said he just randomly made "off the wall" comments, hid in their bedroom, and lied about his whereabouts. He would allow Roberta to care for Osnel, David, Sylvio, and Thomas, but would not allow the boys in the house, forcing them to sleep in the yard.

Weeks went by and the young man continued to exhibit unusual behavior. It was during this time Roberta was convinced he was laying the groundwork to have his family and friends do away with her. Because she believed the Lord's church should live transparently and above reproach, which was contrary to the secrets the preacher kept in his own life, he thought she was a threat to his work.

One night a neighbor man came screaming --- he had found a baby in an outdoor toilet. Roberta rushed to help. The frantic man crawled down into the hole full of human waste and lifted the infant up into Roberta's waiting arms. She desperately wiped feces away from the infant's mouth and nose and immediately took the baby home and bathed her several times to rid the odor. She loved the newborn immediately.

Her husband refused to let her keep the baby. They rarely fought or exchanged harsh words, but that night he cursed and yelled. Through the next weeks, rumors surfaced that Roberta's husband was the father. The mother had tried to get rid of the baby. Even years later, people remember and speak of that evening. Along with his strange behavior in recent months, the birth of the baby undeniably convinced Roberta that her marriage was in grave danger.

The infant was taken in by relatives and Roberta deeply mourned her loss. As she saw the baby at worship each Sunday, she was painfully reminded that she had been denied the opportunity to be a loving mother to an infant who so desperately needed one.

She held a special bond with the baby that deepened. Eventually, the little one was old enough to reach out for Roberta or run to her, receiving a sharp pinch as punishment from her caretaker. Roberta was warned not to talk to the child or in any way show attention; to do so would bring punishment for the little one. As years went by, the child would whisper in Roberta's ear about beatings and mistreatment, pleading to go home with Roberta.

There was nothing legally to be done. Roberta's pain was obvious to the caregivers and they offered the child as a prize to her in exchange for divorcing her husband and returning to the States. That didn't happen.

The young preacher's condition continued to deteriorate. He quit preaching and had young men preach in his stead. He slept on a cot under the banana trees or curled in a fetal position on the floor. He said he heard his dead father talking. He quit bathing and cutting his hair and he was afraid of eating. In retrospect, Roberta realized she should have recognized warning signs early on in their relationship, but at the time she was oblivious to them.

After a while, his strange behavior became evident to others. The elders in the States were called and they tried to counsel long distance, but to no avail. Two of the elders traveled to Santo to give counsel and decided the couple needed to return to Amory for professional help.

In January 2000, they returned to the States and Roberta's husband began seven months of counseling. Despite counseling and visits with psychiatric personnel, his behavior remained unstable. They returned to Haiti in August and he became increasingly violent. He began sleeping with a machete under his pillow to protect himself from Satan. It made Roberta's blood run cold when she discovered he believed her to be Satan. She slept in another room with the door locked.

Roberta left him in November 2000 and financial support from the Amory church ceased. The young preacher left the church and moved to the States the following month. Satan had all but succeeded in destroying an energized, vibrant church with his lies, temptations, and cunning ways.

Many, many people suffered besides these two young people who had great plans for bringing the hope of Christ into a part of the world where there is so little hope. Osnel suffered, as did Thomas, Sylvio, and David. Even though the preacher wouldn't allow the four little boys to sleep in his house, they continued to look hopelessly up to him and would have chosen to stay with him, had it been their choice to make.

The Santo church suffered disillusionment and devastation. Roberta believed her husband had been "the most educated, dynamic, dedicated preacher Haiti had ever had". People's hearts had been touched and the church grew. But because a lot of people were converted to the preacher rather than to Christ, many left. The Santo congregation still exists today but remains small.

The Amory church suffered. It is difficult to always make the wisest decisions, especially concerning a ministry located across the ocean. Roberta received many letters from members who were confused about the right thing to do. One of the older sisters in the Amory church continued to send Roberta $50 a month until her own death several years ago. This money was all Roberta received during her financial drought the first year after she left Robert.

The elders provided wise counsel and Jean and Paul Dickerson gave their unconditional love which covered the couple like a warm blanket. Roberta asked me to thank the Amory church for their confidence in sending them to Haiti in the first place and for their faithful, generous support for over three years.

Roberta suffered. Satan attacked her marriage and the church, and seemingly took control. There were many emotional scars from the four-year marriage, but she now felt relief when the daily threat of violence was no longer present. She had been truly afraid of her ex-husband.

This began a one-year drought period in her life --- financially, emotionally, and mentally, Roberta was drained. She and her parents were still estranged. Although her friends in the States loved and cared about her and remained her prayer warriors, overseas communication technology was terribly lacking. She felt alone, broke, and had four little boys who depended on her.

Roberta had been in Haiti for only a little over four years --- not long enough for the average person to claim a new country as one's own, especially while also feeling such loyalty to America. After the challenges of learning to live as a Haitian, the erratic and threatening behavior of her husband, and all her resources gone, who would blame her if she returned to her roots in the United States? She had two job offers to lure her back, but she prayed the Lord would make a way for her to stay with the four boys. For Roberta, leaving was not an option. She had children who would once again experience abandonment if she packed her bags and left.

Roberta learned what it felt like to have everything stripped away. She had little resources or networking capabilities in Haiti. She had no housing, no money, and little food.

She literally had no place else to go but to Him, her Father. God wants each of us to see all we need is Him. In a way far deeper than most of us experience, Roberta learned what is feels like to be totally dependent on Him. She had no money to trust, no people to trust, no job to trust, no house to trust. All her trust was in her Father and Savior. For Roberta, God was enough. She was just where God wanted her --- where he wants each of us: seeking Him and Him only.

Many of you reading these pages have heard Roberta say, "God will provide." She never said it lightly. *She knew He would.* He always did. Maybe not in her timing, maybe not in the same way she imagined, but always in His perfect timing and in ways that were "abundantly more than she could ask or imagine". She dearly loved seeing how He would surprise her.

God did provide and He did surprise her, over and over in the months and years to come.

Roberta and the kids found a place to stay with Debbie, a friend in the area who operated an orphanage and school. Debbie paid her $100 a week to teach her children English.

While at Debbie's, an unidentified woman came for a short stay. Roberta told me of her --- someone who had once lived in Haiti and who will surely recognize herself here. Roberta's experience of fear, stress, strain, and displacement with four children had taken its toll and she needed someone to take care of her for a few days. This young woman showed up unexpectedly and took her to the Dominican Republic for several days while the children stayed with Debbie. In the Dominican, she wept, slept, and "just was". God provided.

After staying three months with Debbie, Roberta cashed in her life insurance policy and rented a little house at Santo 15. (Santo 15 was Roberta's address, revealing the town name and road number on which she lived.) Roberta continued teaching English at the orphanage to pay for food.

She began her day at 5:00 a.m. as she left home to buy the day's food from local vendors or small shops along the streets. Her little house had little electricity, which meant stifling rooms with no fans to move the smothering air and pesky mosquitoes. Total darkness enveloped them when the sun sank behind the mountains. Roberta and the kids sat out on the steps at night, telling stories and singing until the house cooled off enough to sleep.

Though in dire straits herself, desperate people still begged her to take their children, and not many weeks went by before she had six more children join her family in the small house at Santo 15.

A father of six knocked on the gate --- the oldest three were in the hospital and he wanted Roberta to take the three healthiest ones, all of whom were suffering from malnutrition: Woody (pronounced Woodsey) (12), Richard (9), and Shelda (7). She told him she couldn't take all three but made an appointment on a street corner the next day to meet the father with one of his children. He appeared with all three children and said, "Pick one." All three went home with Roberta.

The three siblings became fluent in English and served as translators in Roberta's home and are still asked to help when present day medical teams arrive in Haiti.

The next young lady Roberta brought into her home was Spangle (pronounced Spang), whom she knew from the Santo church, where Roberta continued to worship. Her father was a voodoo priest and her stepmother was a Jehovah's Witness. When Spangle was 16 years old, she was baptized and became active in the church and helped Roberta teach the younger children.

Before he left Haiti and traveled to the States, Roberta's former husband and Spangle's sister became involved in an affair. Spangle did not tell Roberta of the affair, but her family insisted she had. Consequently, Spangle was kicked out of her family's house and forced to sleep in an abandoned car until Roberta invited her to live with her family. Spangle now has her own business, located in the same neighborhood as the Sonlight Children's Home.

Soon after Spangle got settled in, a Christian couple from the church brought a very pregnant woman to Roberta's gate --- she wanted Roberta to take the child when it was born. Roberta agreed and took the young woman to all her doctor appointments and made sure she had food. In January of 2002, Marie came into this world, weighing a whopping ten pounds.

Caring for a newborn in Haiti is vastly different from the way it's done in America and the other children did not understand all the fuss about sterilizing bottles and water or why the umbilical cord had to be protected and cleaned thoroughly. They didn't understand much of anything about sanitation. Roberta felt like these precautions caused the other children in the home to resent the time, energy, and money spent on this new baby.

After Marie's birth, Kerlange and her brother, Pierre, were the last additions to Roberta's household at Santo 15. They lived in St. Marc, Haiti, before their mother sent them to the big city of Port-au-Prince for education, opportunity, and to get them away from their father, a voodoo priest.

They lived with their aunt who couldn't afford to feed them. In late 2001, the aunt had a baby and Kerlange (12) helped her deliver. Two hours after the birth, the aunt died. Kerlange and Pierre (eight) went back to St. Marc for the

Roberta

funeral, but in four months the children were back in Santo, waiting at Roberta's gate. Pierre's hair was red and straight and Kerlange's coloring was off, tell-tale signs of extreme malnutrition.

Having never had enough food to eat, the two siblings thoroughly enjoyed the food in Roberta's home. Not only was there enough to fill their tummies, but it tasted delicious. That was probably the only part of the adjustment into the new family that was easy for the two young siblings. Kerlange had taken care of Pierre since she was five years old and Pierre was nine months old. Essentially, she was his mother. She lived with a burden of fear much of the time, anxious that this active baby boy would injure himself and she would be blamed.

Even so, relinquishing her motherly responsibilities to another woman was threatening to her and to Pierre, who had come to expect Kerlange to take care of him and fulfill his every whim. Roberta insisted Pierre do what he could for himself and his discipline should come through her, not Kerlange.

Kerlange had never felt loved before and as she moved into a totally unfamiliar environment, it caused her to retreat deeper into herself and she talked very little. It helped that Kerlange and Shelda became good friends and over time she softened toward her new mom. She enjoyed the Bible studies in Proverbs which started each day and the devotionals which ended the day. Kerlange especially enjoyed the times when the girls gathered for an afternoon read-aloud of a favored book I brought from the States.

First Family Photo at Santo 15
Back Left: Spangle, Sylvio, Thomas, David, Roberta and
Marie
Front Left: Shelda, Woody, Richard

Chapter 10
Help, Hope, and Healing

God never asks anything of us that He doesn't equip us to do. In Roberta's case, she needed to be equipped with love, encouragement, manpower, and finances. Help was on the way.

Before we knew Roberta, my sister, Louine Woodroof, and her late husband, Jim, met a young man, Norm Curington, in Canada at the end of 2001. It wasn't long until they made the connection that Norm lived a mere ten minutes from our home in Palm Beach Gardens, FL. A few days later Norm was sitting at our dining room table, listening to our stories of Haiti.

Norm was a successful businessman with a heart for God. For years, he had been setting aside monies to be used for God --- he just had not figured out the recipient. My husband, David, had a heart for Haiti. Soon we were all off on the adventure of our lifetimes.

Within a few weeks, David took Norm and his mom, Ruth Curington, to Cap Haitien, the only part of Haiti familiar to my husband. Because changing airports in Port-au-Prince can be tricky, the missionaries in Cap Haitien asked Roberta to help the group on their return trip. Roberta picked them up, checked to see if they were hungry (Norm was), and took them to a gas station that also sold sandwiches. Since Norm had no Haitian money, Roberta bought him a burger. Weeks later we learned it was her last five dollars.

Roberta

When David got home, he said, "I have met the most amazing woman I have ever known. You have to come and see." We started making plans.

In the spring of 2002, following three years of drought for Roberta, the elders of the Estes church of Christ in Henderson, TN, called to interview Roberta at the urging of Jesse Robertson. Jesse was the young college student who, several years ago, helped Roberta's ex-husband get into Freed Hardeman University. As the elders listened with anticipation, Roberta shared her immediate goals: get the Nutrition Center up and running again, educate her children, and start women's classes. She thanked God for His providence in bringing people she didn't know, but who knew her, to partner with her in this ministry.

From the onset, the elders adopted a hands-on approach with their support efforts. They traveled regularly to Port-au-Prince and brought Roberta home as they nurtured and advised her. Jesse became a liaison, effectively guiding the communication between Roberta and the Estes church. He traveled at least annually to Haiti to lead medical mission teams, stayed abreast of the work in Santo and its neighbors, and stay informed of Roberta's needs.

The following November, we invited Roberta to join Norm, David, me, and other fellow travelers, in Cap Haitien for Thanksgiving dinner. I was giddy with anticipation of meeting this woman. Missionaries David and Sarah Dirrim, Dr. Mark and Cathy Pearson, Ron and Dianna Cyphers, and their families helped us enjoy a smoked turkey and all the trimmings, which we brought from the States.

We flew directly in and out of Cap Haitien on Missionary Flights International, a non-profit organization aiding missionaries in Haiti and other close islands. They do a phenomenal job keeping the servants who are working in these areas connected to their loved ones, supplied with their needs, and encouraged.

A Clay Jar Too Soon Broken

When Roberta arrived, she was quiet and reserved, seemingly on her guard, unsure of why we all had gathered. Those of you who knew her are probably scratching your heads. "Roberta, quiet?" you say?

Norm asked her what kind of help she needed; she avoided the question until it was time to return home. After such a long time of no substantial assistance until the Estes church approached her five months earlier, she was guarded about anticipating more help could be on the way. As Roberta was quick to admit, she had a "chip on her shoulder".

She finally told him she needed peanut butter, oatmeal, and vitamins for the Nutrition Center. Cathy teased Roberta about not knowing how to make a proper list and proceeded to show her how to ask for help: kitchen supplies, generator, meat for her children, linens, chocolate chips for cookies, etc.

In December, Norm called and asked if he could bring Christmas presents for the children. He not only provided gifts for the children, but also a generator, an inverter, and batteries. This was Roberta's first taste of almost 24 hours of electricity. Between the wear and tear of Haiti's dirt and grit on equipment and the cost of diesel to run the generator, around the clock electricity turned out to be an unrealistic luxury.

After enjoying the gifts and a great visit, a thankful Roberta put Norm on the plane headed back to Florida, not expecting to hear from him again.

He surprised her. He was back in January, brought more food and snacks, and told her he planned to be back in April to look for land on which to build a permanent home. In the meantime, he asked Roberta to look for suitable property. Roberta never looked --- he couldn't be serious.

David and I traveled to Port-au-Prince the following March to meet Roberta's children and see where they lived. We were astounded to find she and the eleven children were living in a tiny house, along with a young American woman, Rachel Schwartz. Rachel, a member of the Estes church, came to help for a year.

Norm Curington and Marie

Roberta and Rachel graciously and sacrificially gave up their bed for David and me. The next morning, noticing all the bedrooms had been filled with children, I asked where the two of them had slept. They pointed to the plywood boards balanced over chairs in the tiny living room. I was humbled, horrified, and ashamed, all at the same time.

Norm, David, and I returned the next month and managed to find a house with a security wall. Beacon Light Ministries, a non-profit organization recently formed by Norm, bought the house and property.

A Clay Jar Too Soon Broken

Roberta freely gave her last $5 to feed a stranger and God blessed her "immeasurably more than she could ask or imagine". She was in a stupor. Things moved so quickly, she found it difficult to process.

Norm brought Roberta to West Palm Beach and took her on a shopping spree at Home Depot for appliances, tile, toilets, etc. Next, many teams of workers, mostly from the Palm Beach Lakes Church of Christ in Palm Beach Gardens, FL, arrived to make the house livable. Jesse and his dad put on their tool belts and partnered with one of the teams.

The team in November 2004 attacked tough jobs. They corrected improper wiring, broke up concrete floors and re-cemented them, and reworked substandard PVC pipe filled with concrete. Norm taught Roberta and her kids how to tile their floors and they were quick studies.

While the men and a few women worked on the new house, my friend, Sandy DeVall, and I cooked Thanksgiving dinner. What a feat! It was stifling hot, so we propped the kitchen door open, only to welcome in swarms of flies. When we couldn't stand the flies any longer, we closed the door and Sandy became our number one fly-squasher. About the time the flies were killed off, it was unbearably hot again and the cycle repeated itself.

The oven was either on or off and it cooked at 500 degrees only. Somehow the feast turned out well and was appreciated by all, especially the children.

Many small teams worked on Roberta's house for the next two years. One man must be singled out. Sandy's husband, Bob, was an electrician who had never been out of the country, much less to a third world country. Bob began each day with a prayer asking God to show him who he could help and how he could help them. When the call came to help with Roberta's house, he was first to volunteer. Bob worked tirelessly for the original five days and then said he needed another week. Completely out of his comfort zone, he remained alone in Haiti to finish his job for Roberta. To our great sorrow, a few weeks later, Bob died on his job after collapsing from a heart attack while on a ladder in Florida.

Roberta and her children moved into their new place, even as renovation continued. The additional space and no rent payment made up for any construction inconveniences.

The new home was named Sonlight Children's Home by Roberta. She was adamant that it was a children's home and not an orphanage. In Haiti, the staff in orphanages go home at night, a nighttime crew replacing them. Roberta lived with her children around the clock and raised them as her own. There was no magic age when they had to leave their home.

Roberta's House

Front Gate

Shelda, Pierre, and Ashimetre Painting the House

Using the horticultural skills her mother taught her, Roberta and the children tackled the rock-filled, hard dirt that was their yard. They moved rocks for days and then transformed the barren land by planting palm trees, coconut trees, and lovely bougainvillea. The bougainvillea eventually cascaded over and softened the harsh cement security walls, hiding the razor wire used for security. In the center of the front yard, they planted a Plumeria tree and formed a wide circle of large stones around the base of the trunk. The heady fragrance of the yellow blossoms and the shade from its leaves on far-reaching branches invited many a conversation, tree-climber, or photo opportunity.

As the years passed, the chasm in the relationship between Roberta and her parents became smaller. Time and life are great healers. After the family moved into their new home, her mom and dad traveled twice to see Roberta and to meet the children. They also began keeping in touch by phone and Roberta made trips to their home, helping in ways that were now difficult for her aging parents.

After the move into the big house, Roberta's family continued to grow. Fellow church member Renel and her son, Francky (pronounced Franky), gently held the hands of five-year-old Achimetre (pronounced Ash-she-met) as they brought him to Roberta. His downcast eyes were caked with a yellowish material that obscured his vision. He had open slits at the corners of his mouth and at his earlobes, causing the lobes to separate from his ears. His ashen skin was pitted with sores and he was malnourished.

Roberta made plans to take Achimetre to the doctor with his mom. When they didn't show up, she went looking for him. She found Achimetre and his sister locked out of the house, sleeping on rice sacks in the mud. They had no clothes or shoes. Roberta took him to the pediatrician who wouldn't touch him. She tried a second doctor, who also was of no help.

Haitians have very little, but they each have a body. If that body is flawed, the person often has nothing. Such was the case with sweet Achimetre --- a social outcast because an unknown disease had left his body looking as though he had leprosy. One Sunday morning, when Achimetre was not allowed to sit with the other children in Bible class, Pierre took his hand and sat with him under a nearby tree. When Roberta became aware of Achimetre's shunning, the whole family left and walked home together. It was a huge proclamation of love and acceptance for a little boy who had never known either.

When the medical team came the following month in March, Dr. Rachel Wyatt, Doctor of Optometry, accurately diagnosed Achimetre with herpes, transmitted from his mom during his birth. With proper medical treatment, he has grown into a handsome young man and has moved to Florida, hoping to finish his education. He is smart and has a good heart.

Pierre and Achimetre

Ben was 14 months old when he was brought by his mother to Roberta's in 2004 in hopes of a better life. He and Marie quickly became best buds since they were close in age. Ben thrived with Roberta's family until his mother returned for him two years later, concerned that Roberta would not teach him Creole. Ben was emaciated, his hair was red, and his eyes sunk back in his head when his mother finally returned him to Sonlight a few months later. Upon his return, Ben declared he was "here to stay" and would never live with his birth mother again.

Roberta

Ben

The assurance of being fed every day is powerful; in Haiti, children equate full tummies with love. Roberta's desire was to go beyond filling their tummies. She wanted to also fill their hearts with the love of Jesus, creating in them a desire to be the light and salt in this dark world.

First Photo After Move to New House
Back: Thomas;
Middle: Ben, Woody, Kerlange, Sylvio, David, Roberta, Marie
Front: Pierre, Shelda, Achimetre, Richard

A Clay Jar Too Soon Broken

A year after Ben moved in, Michemana (pronounced Mish-mana) came from Gonaives, Haiti, several hours' drive north of Port-au-Prince. Her father was alive but never around and she lived with her mom and older sister. Always sickly, the dimpled little girl suffered with breathing issues and a lack of energy but was never diagnosed or treated.

Her mom sought help for Michemana through a voodoo priest. She allowed him to traumatize this little girl with acts of frightening, potentially fatal, atrocities involving blood, a live chicken, and odorous water. Michemana's symptoms worsened.

After her mother died, eight-year-old Michemana and her sister were sent to live with their aunt and her four children in a one-room cement house with a tin roof. There was little food. Michemana was designated to purchase water in a five-gallon container which balanced on her head. Her sister was sent away to an uncle's house to be a restavek. Though Michemana's sister could not come back to visit, Michemana went to her lonely sister on occasions --- the two little girls shared many hugs and stories.

One morning rain came down in torrents, deep water collecting in front of her house. With help, Michemana climbed a tree for safety until it fell; her uncle then got her to higher ground. This was the beginning of the 2004 Gonaives floods with powerful mud slides carrying every home in its path to the sea, killing several thousand people.

After the flood, Michemana, now ten years old, came to live at Sonlight and was promptly diagnosed with asthma. That same day she was given medicine and for the first time in her life, she breathed freely.

Here is an excerpt from her letter to a friend when Michemana was about 13 years old:

> "For the first time in my life, I heard about Jesus. I learned about being a family and living together with people. I learned about not being ungrateful. It was

at my mom's house that I first told God thank you for saving my life in the floods. I have the opportunity to get a good education. I didn't realize how much I didn't know, but now I am grateful for the chance God has given me to learn so many new things.

"When I came to my mom's, she made everyone in the house work. I used to hate to work. I thought she was making me a slave. Now, I see that work is a good thing. It will help me when I get older so I can live. I also learned that when I do something bad, my mom punishes me because she loves me and wants to help me. I didn't know what 'time out' was. I never had that in Gonaives but now understand what it means. In May of 2005, I gave my life to Christ, and was baptized into His body."

A month after the earthquake in 2010, Michemana grew rebellious. At age 15, she decided to return to her extended family in Gonaives. She was home for a couple of years, growing and maturing and contemplating what she was missing at Sonlight: her mom, her siblings, and the precious gift of an education.

Before going back to Gonaives, Michemana loved Roberta but didn't have a great relationship with her. Mostly she saw Roberta as an authority figure and a means to an end. With Roberta in her life, life would be easier. Upon her return as a 17-year-old, she found herself looking at her mom through clearer eyes, bonding with her, and developing a deep love for her she never thought possible. She now meant it, in every way, when she called Roberta "Mom".

Closely following Michemana, eight-year-old Guerline (pronounced Gere-leen) moved into Roberta's home. Her mentally ill mother died soon after she gave birth to Guerline. Neighbors tried to keep the baby alive until family members arrived from Mirebalais. At three years of age, she was brought to a girls' orphanage in Santo. After five years, the director asked Roberta to take Guerline because she did not fit in at the girls' orphanage.

Guerline was catatonic, silent, and walked only when someone held her hand. It took two months in Roberta's home before she spoke openly. Even today she is uncommonly shy in talking about herself. However, now in her early twenties in 2019, Guerline is fluent in English, highly skilled in translating for the medical or other mission teams, and is a good cook.

Not long after Guerline was added to the Sonlight family, Kerline (pronounced Care-leen) arrived. In their growing up years, Kerline and her sister spent many nights walking the streets looking for their mother. Each night found them sleeping somewhere different than the night before. Though the girls were neglected, they were very intelligent, ranking first and second in their classes.

Even as she lived on the streets, Kerline was pulled toward God and His church. At 14 years of age, she was baptized and came to live with Roberta and her children, still struggling with the guilt of her past lifestyle. Each time Roberta tried to get close to her, she'd run away.

After a couple of years, Kerline left Sonlight, only to return in 18 months with a baby girl, Rosie, in tow. Ricardo, her boyfriend and father of the baby, also accompanied her. Ricardo loved her and wanted to marry her, but Kerline would not. Ricardo eventually became the caretaker of the Guest House and Kerline started her own laundry products business. Mom and dad shared custody of Rosie.

Shortly after these new teenagers came to live at Sonlight, Renel brought a second throw-away-child. This time the child was literally thrown away on a garbage heap. Renel and Francky discovered the newborn covered with ants and Francky quickly removed his shirt, using it to brush the ants from the baby. Renel had no means to keep him and brought the baby to the only woman she knew who could and would love him.

93

Roberta

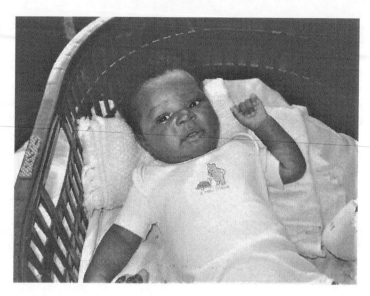

Paul David

After the baby arrived at her gate, Roberta immediately took him to be checked out by a doctor. Amazingly, he was healthy and thriving, but that would soon change.

A few months later, on a Thursday afternoon, a young woman, who had eaten at the Nutrition Center for years, made an appearance in Roberta's home. For safety reasons, she had not been allowed in Roberta's home previously, but suddenly she was there and, as she passed through, picked up Paul David, held him for seconds, and put him down again. The woman left immediately and within a couple of hours the infant screamed in pain and had breathing difficulties. Friday and Saturday, Roberta frantically sought help for the baby as she went to numerous hospitals and clinics that either turned him away or did not have equipment necessary to diagnose and treat him. By Saturday afternoon, with blood coming from his bowels, Roberta desperately tried to find someone to do an ultrasound, draw blood for lab work, give him oxygen, and start an IV. Oxygen tanks were finally found at one hospital, but alas, they were empty. An IV couldn't be started for the lack of equipment. He died.

A Clay Jar Too Soon Broken

At worship the next morning, the same young woman who had picked up the baby a few days ago, boldly walked up and asked Roberta if Paul David had died yet. Roberta believed the woman poisoned the infant as an act of revenge for some perceived affront.

Roberta picked out Paul David's burial clothes and she and 18-year-old Thomas took them to the morgue to dress him. The horrific final blow was about to land. The cooler at the morgue in the hospital was not working and ants were eating the baby's eyes. Thomas dressed the infant; Roberta had no more strength.

Roberta and the children buried Paul David in a special place in their backyard.

Later that year, Francky came to live at Sonlight. His mom and dad separated and he developed behavioral problems. He is a capable young man who spent a lot of time working on Roberta's vehicles.

Part III: Shaping Children for the Future

"They may not have my eyes. They may not have my smile, but they have all my heart."

- Unknown

Chapter 11
"How Do You Decide, Roberta?"

Eighteen children were now living at the Sonlight Children's Home. Hundreds more outside the gate needed a safe place to live.

"So how do you decide, Roberta, who you take in and who you turn away?" That's a question I asked, as I know countless others have as well. The need for safe, nurturing homes for children too many to number was, and still is, urgent in Haiti. Daily, desperate mothers or fathers knocked on her gate, begging Roberta to take in their starving children. Sometimes an infant was brought because the young mother had died, was dying, or was just too sick to care for the baby and no relatives available to step in. Still other babies and children were brought to Roberta by relatives who were church members.

The children ranged from newborns fighting for their lives to older children whose parent didn't know how to keep them safe from the streets as they foraged food. It was always basically the same issue: food to keep them alive. No matter their ages, they were all skin and bones with classic signs of starvation.

Her answer to my question: "I pray over this child and listen to my gut." Translated, that means she tried to listen to what God was showing her. Most mothers don't want to give up their children; they just want them to live. Roberta's priority was to keep the family intact, so she gave the mother enough food to survive for a few days. She also gave the mother shoes, shirts, or dresses out of the latest huge container she had received from the States, in hopes it would help the mother jumpstart a business to sustain her and the children for a longer length of time, perhaps permanently.

If something more than food was needed to remedy the situation, Roberta listened for the voice deep inside her. If she didn't feel an overwhelming, compelling sense of need to take the child, with a heavy heart, she refused the child.

This voice inside her got a real workout during the next few years, from about 2006 to 2009 --- 12 new children joined the Sonlight family.

2006 was the year that her 45-year-old brother died unexpectedly in the States. He died from health issues, but it was especially heart-wrenching because he was missing two months before his body was discovered. As Roberta was accepting these twelve new children into her home over the next several months and years, she was also needed in the States to comfort and assist her grieving parents. This was not the last time she would feel so torn and stretched to be two places at once.

But no matter Roberta's circumstances, the children kept coming.

The next six children came between 2006 and 2008. I have little biographical information on these young people, nor did I know them well. But they were members of the family and deserve to be included.

Darline is in her late 20's in 2019 and probably came to Sonlight toward the end of 2006. After leaving Sonlight, she returned to work for Roberta periodically in various ways. She has given birth to three children.

Mackendy (pronounced MacKenzie) is trying to finish high school. He speaks fluent English and translates in the clinics.

Judith, the sister of Marchodson, moved in and lived there most of the time, going home on occasion. During her growing up years she was a hard worker and good friends with Michemana. Judith has moved to the States.

Yvena, along with Guerline, came from the girls' orphanage mentioned earlier. Interested and gifted in hair styling, Yvena enrolled in beauty classes with Roberta's help.

Bettina and Natalie, quiet young girls, came to live with Roberta about the same time and stayed for a relatively short time.

Wiles (pronounced Willis), about 19 years of age in 2019, arrived in 2006. His father was not around, his mother was too old to sell herself anymore, and she had no other means to support her son. An American from Alaska met Wiles and brought him to Roberta. He was a studious young man who not only wanted to finish school but was seeking God's truth. When he found the truth, he wanted to share it with other people who had not yet heard.

He helped lead the family devotionals, taught at teen retreats, and his heart was big and tender as he looked for ways to serve. When Roberta took the older children to the

Wiles

nursing home to bring smiles to the elderly, she often found Wiles engaged in conversation with one of the residents or wiping an old man's dripping mouth.

Not long after Wiles' arrival, a whirlwind came to take residence in the Sonlight Children's Home, disguised as 14-year-old Mirlande. There is much mystery to Mirlande's story, but we know she was raised in the States, reportedly was an honor student, and she spoke no Creole. For reasons unknown, she was sent to live with her dad in Port-au-Prince, where Mirlande's passport and visa were confiscated and destroyed, complicating a return to the States.

Her father asked Roberta to take Mirlande into her home to finish her education. A still, small voice was telling Roberta to decline. She didn't listen and "all hell broke loose" for the next three years.

After she moved into Sonlight, it was discovered Mirlande's papers were false and she had lived in New York with people making an illegal living. She was sent to Miami to live with an uncle who, in turn, sent her to Haiti. Mirlande is a charismatic, bright young woman whose past had a stronghold on her. She never integrated into life at Roberta's house.

Mirlande has a younger step-sister, Natacha, who shared the same mother. Natacha's father contracted AIDS and asked Roberta to take Natacha, age seven, into her home. She stayed for a year and then returned to her parents.

Around the time of Wiles and Mirlande's addition to the home, Roberta received a container with a huge supply of formula. She was puzzled since she had no infants and there were none in her sights. But God had a plan and was working it. Daniel was 15 days old and had malaria when he arrived at Sonlight. His mother and father were members of a neighboring church in Bonnet. His mom had a stroke when he was born, leaving her completely paralyzed. Daniel's grandmother, a voodoo priestess, agreed to take care of him. When Daniel's father found him on a voodoo altar, he stole Daniel away and brought him to Roberta for safety. The baby was covered with sores and didn't look like he had been washed since birth.

Roberta hadn't had a baby in the house since four-year-old Marie was born. Although she had not been preparing for another baby, Roberta believed God had --- Daniel had plenty of milk to nurture his weak, sore-ridden body. She had many stories like this one to share, stories about how God was always there, working in ways that puzzled her, stunned her, and made her smile.

She laughingly told of all the love and hugs Daniel received. She had read somewhere that new babies need '50 kisses and a 100 hugs' a day. With his tummy full and his heart filled with love from his new family, Daniel stabilized immediately and began sleeping all night at two months of age. At three years of age, he could dribble a basketball as big as he was and steal sideways glances at the same time - just to be sure you were looking!

Just a couple of months after Daniel settled in, Joseph was brought to the home at 21 days old. He also came with malaria and had the addition of voodoo amulets around his neck and wrists. His mother died a few days after his birth, her ninth pregnancy. Word on the street was that his father had five other women and was not around to take care of this baby. Joseph's 18-year-old brother kept him alive by feeding him sugar-water.

When Roberta first laid eyes on him, she did not think Joseph would survive. He cried silently, no sound uttering from his mouth. He arrived at 11:00 on a Friday morning and she implemented the same regime she had used for Daniel: '50 kisses, 100 hugs', and formula. Joseph was only able to take a half to one ounce at a time. By nighttime, he had not yet urinated. She watched him all night to see if he was still breathing. All day Saturday, still no wet diaper. Roberta took him to worship Sunday morning and still no wet diaper. Sunday night at 11:00, a wet diaper! His kidneys were working and they all celebrated.

Roberta

Roberta now had four-year-old Marie, two-month-old Daniel, and newborn Joseph sleeping in her bed --- she didn't get a lot of sleep.

After the two infants arrived, the sixth child was added in 2007. Lofane (pronounced Lo-fon) was 16 years old when he moved in for a couple of years. He and his sister, Woodleyne, were some of the first children Roberta met in her new neighborhood back when Lofane was only four years old in 1996. He couldn't speak English and Roberta couldn't speak Creole, but their hearts connected. He was a sweet boy living in abject poverty.

His father left home at 4:30 a.m. He locked the door behind him and left the naked children outside. His job of pulling a cart in the marche (market) was considered the lowliest of jobs in Haiti. It bore a stigma which shamed the family. At the end of the day, his father would bring home two or three sweet potatoes, providing the only meal of the day for his family.

Unknown Man Pulling a Cart

Roberta brought them clothes to wear, but the father locked them in the house to "save" them. Between their nakedness and their father's lowly job, the children endured great ridicule.

One of Roberta's fondest memories of Lofane was when she sat under the mango tree and read "The Creation" or "Noah's Ark" in English to him. They did this for a couple of years and Lofane began to excel in school --- it gave him confidence that he could learn.

Lofane

Roberta taught Lofane how to become a peacemaker. When there was a fight at school, he was able to calm the troublemakers down and say, "Let's talk about it." The director of the school saw this and was impressed, especially since oftentimes these incidents ended in the shaking of hands. All fights in the Sonlight home ultimately ended in the shaking of hands.

In October of the next year, several months after Lofane came to join the family, Mike was brought to Roberta because his mother had huge nodules caused by tuberculosis and was physically unable to care for Mike, three months old. He was in good health and had a big appetite. Because he was strong-willed, it took Roberta two months to train him to sleep all night.

When Mike was nine months old, his mother came back to get him, traumatizing all his new brothers and sisters and hurting Roberta's heart. His mother thought she wanted him, but in three days she brought him back, demanding $3000 and a US visa for the father. Roberta wisely did not give in to her demands.

Nine-year-old Mack moved into Sonlight the following year. He had been raised in an American-operated orphanage that was closing. Mack chose to come to Roberta's house because of the tales he heard from her older boys while they all attended a Vacation Bible School. He was a good boy, very mature and compliant, obeying immediately with a good attitude. He spoke great English and was pleased he was allowed to speak Creole, something he had not been able to do at the orphanage.

Mack is a self-motivated young man who responded well to homeschooling at Sonlight. He has shown himself invaluable in translating for clinics, Bible lessons and sermons on Sunday morning, and for visiting instructors at the International School of Theology. He has moved out of Sonlight into a place provided by sponsors as he attends a Haitian school. Mack's desire is to finish his education in America.

Along with Mack, from the same orphanage, came 15-year-old Nicky. DeeDee, director of the orphanage, rescued him from a garbage heap where his father had thrown him, believing that Nicky was the result of his wife sleeping with Satan. Nicky was an albino.

His albinism was not what defined him as a person in the Sonlight family. Though he lived at Sonlight a mere two months before he died in the earthquake, he made a special place for himself in the heart of each member of Roberta's family.

Shortly before the earthquake, Nicky made the comment to Roberta, "I've finally found a home." He was intelligent and loved nature; the children called him the "bird whisperer". He had a strong spirit and Roberta always felt she was in the presence of somebody special, "like he was from a different time and place". She often prayed that God would show her how to help him become a productive Christian man.

And still the family continued to grow and in a big way, though Roberta was not looking for any more babies. Babies are energy-draining, time-consuming, and heart-stealers. Her infants were now toddlers and stabilized in their health. God had other plans.

Two-month-old twin boys, Micah and Luke, arrived in February 2009, 11 months before the earthquake. Their mother had been living under a tree during the rainy season with the babies. She was in a relationship with a man who didn't want the baggage of babies.

Micah is the oldest and weighed 4 lbs. 6 oz., while Luke weighed in at 8 lbs. Luke had malaria but no underlying health issues. He was a crier and consequently was nursed the most to quiet him. Micah, on the other hand, was sickly and frail. Every breath was a struggle and anything he ate, he threw up. The Haitian doctors diagnosed him with malaria, typhoid fever, and double pneumonia. Roberta bought soymilk, feeding him frequent small meals, but the poor infant just lay there.

In March, the Estes church sent yet another medical team down. After examining him, Scott Miskelly, nurse practitioner, was doubtful Micah could survive and told Roberta to "get ready". But Micah did survive and, at four months old, cataracts were discovered in both eyes. A huge fund-raiser took place in Henderson to raise the $30,000 needed. College students at Freed-Hardeman University raised $7,000 in a single collection! Roberta secured a visa for Micah, a truly exasperating experience in and of itself. When Micah was nine months old, the two traveled to Memphis, TN, for his surgery where they were hosted by Rachel and Joshua Wyatt.

His tiny lens and cataracts were removed and surgery went well. Plans were made to return when Micah turned six or seven years of age to replace the lens. As Roberta went to pay the bills, they said, "No charge." The doctor fitted him with "bottle" glasses, frames with extremely thick lenses, and sent him home.

Just over a year ago, at 10 years of age, Micah had his successful lens transplant surgery. The original $30,000 meant for his cataract surgery paid for this last surgery. He is doing well.

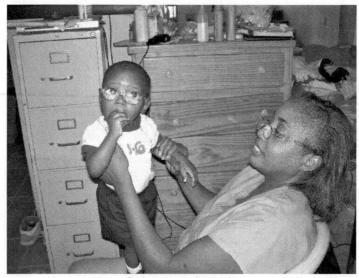

Roberta and Micah

Chapter 12
New Home, New Family, New Routines

Every time a new child entered the family, they were all embraced alike. They integrated and had each other's back. They had the same food, bed, and clothes which helped them feel a part of the family. Each of Roberta's children remembered what it felt like to be the new kid and immediately began helping the newcomer with the process of fitting in.

Even though they were being rescued from a desperate situation, the children still were leaving behind what was familiar to them and were thrust into a new family. There was no easing into this home, filled with lots of brothers and sisters, a new mom, and strange ways of doing things. They puzzled over all the handwashing, questioned why they had to wear shoes outside, and wondered what was up with a chore list? It was frightening and safe, all at the same time.

Routines were established that necessitated change. For example, the children had to learn to use the toilet instead of a tree or wetting their beds. The practice of using toilet paper was also new to them. When a child first arrived, he usually found it difficult to believe breakfast was not the only meal of the day, but he would have two more meals before he slept that night. Sometimes it was weeks, if not months, before the children stopped hoarding food or devouring so much food at a meal that their little bellies revolted and threw it up.

Each child came with basically the same set of issues, but with differing personal reactions. Children react differently to sexual abuse, beatings, starvation, meanness, broken promises, and neglect. Since trust had been dropped and stomped on, it was hard for the children to grasp Roberta truly loved them. They thought she got rich off them, sometimes accusingly telling her, "If it wasn't for us, you wouldn't be given money and clothes."

The children were confronted with a whole new belief system. They had been on the streets or lived with people who had never heard about Jesus, who had no honor code, and who shared no mutual trust. As Roberta struggled to live among a people who did not trust, she discovered many said only what they thought you wanted to hear. They protected themselves by lying and became suspicious when you treated them with kindness and respect. The children who came to live with Roberta had come to own this mentality.

As the children were introduced to Jesus, it took time to process love, forgiveness, and self-sacrificing. The teachings were foreign and counterculture to them.

Slowly a child realized he was indeed safe, he had a family to love him, and he would be fed three times a day. There were still eleven children to come and eventually find such a home at Sonlight.

Three-year-old Magalie experienced shame matched only by Nicky's, the little boy with albinism. She was born with a large cephalocele positioned between her eyes at the top of her nose. Evelyn Boyd, whom Roberta had met soon after becoming a Christian, discovered Magalie in northern Haiti. Three different times Evelyn gave money to preachers to find a doctor for Magalie and all three times the preachers stole the funds for personal use.

A Clay Jar Too Soon Broken

Evelyn contacted Roberta and traveled down to Port-au-Prince with Magalie in tow. A cat scan revealed no brain matter was involved in the growth and if she could get to the States, it could be removed. Magalie was an outcast of society, enduring taunts, stares, and abuse.

Roberta called to see if I could find someone to do this surgery, preferably pro bono. My husband and I live in St. Paul, MN, one and a half hours from the Mayo Clinic in Rochester, MN, which takes a limited amount of charity cases. Many phone calls later we were blessed by the Catholic Social Services to take one of their pro bono slots for Magalie as long as there was no cost to Catholic Social Services. Surgery was set for December 2009, the same year six other children came to live at Sonlight and just a month before the earthquake occurred.

I flew with my friend, Meredith Ekdahl Greenfield, from Stamford, TX, to escort Magalie to Minnesota. Our fears of how this three-year-old would deal with two unknown women, a huge machine called an airplane, and unfamiliar food were unfounded. She was very docile and cooperative, internalizing the fear that had to be hers.

Magalie's surgery took 11 hours with a team which included a neurosurgeon, a plastic surgeon, and a pediatric surgeon. Mayo Clinic treated her as a full-paying member of society and they spoiled her well. After Magalie's discharge, her neurosurgeon called our home twice to check on Magalie's family following the earthquake, just one of many ways the doctors, nurses, and staff demonstrated compassionate and attentive care.

Did I mention it was Christmas? You couldn't find tiny Magalie in the bed for all the donated gifts.

My husband and I spent three weeks with Magalie in the hospital. Stacey Sikes, then director of the House of Compassion in Rochester, MN, was a constant companion to David and me, praying and visiting with us daily. The House of Compassion, a mission of the local Church of Christ, is a much-needed non-profit group which operates three houses to host families of Mayo patients. It is a Godsend for loved ones, giving them a safe, comfortable place to rest, located within walking distance of the Mayo Clinic campus. Families are not charged, though contributions are not refused.

Magalie was in our home a total of five months and we adored her. Winter coats, hats, and mittens puzzled her, and she was mesmerized by the freezing, white stuff that made her fingers cold.

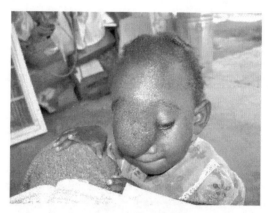

Magalie Before Surgery

Magalie, David, and Charlene After Surgery

A Clay Jar Too Soon Broken

Magalie Today

Near the same time of Magalie's arrival, five-year-old Henri (pronounced "Ahn-ray") became a part of Roberta's family. Roberta liked to tell the story of how she finished praying one day, opened her eyes, looked up, and there stood Henri. Having dropped her off, her father called later to explain that her mother died soon after Henri was born. What he didn't tell her about was the stream of women coming in and out of his house which left no time for Henri. Roberta took her to a friend's home, but Henri ran away to the streets. After she was found, Roberta brought Henri home with her.

Henri is 15 years old in 2019. I have a story that revealed her compassionate character, even at the early age of five. One afternoon, as I read a story to the little children sitting in small chairs in a semicircle, I realized the air no longer smelled fresh. Actually, it was rather pungent due to a little someone's diaper. I was about to ask for assistance from an older child, when Henri arose. She picked up the toddler (almost as big as herself) and went to change the diaper as naturally as if she'd been doing it for years. Since she was in my line of view, I was able to see how gently and thoroughly she changed that dirty diaper. I was awestruck.

Newcomers Magalie and Henri, along with the rest of the family, soon welcomed a new brother, Madochee. Years ago, when the first congregation was started in Santo, Roberta and her husband met a man who washed cars in Port-au-Prince. ("Washing cars" in Haiti means to walk in traffic with a dirty rag in your hand and wipe the dust off the windshield and side windows. Then a hand raps on the window, asking for pay.)

The couple invited him and his girlfriend to come worship with them. They came and eventually Roberta sewed her first wedding dress and baked her first wedding cake for their wedding. This man and woman were the first to be baptized in the new congregation. Their first child died after being birthed on a sidewalk. Their third child was Madochee. As the years went by, the marriage deteriorated and Madochee ended up with many half-siblings from the other men in his mother's life.

The family lived in Cite Soleil, a community near Port au Prince, home to the poorest of the poor. Because of violence in the streets of Port-au-Prince, the father could no longer safely work there, which meant he had no income for his family. Madochee, seven years old, was living with his mother, sleeping on the ground, not eating, and not doing well. His father came to Roberta with reports from neighbors that Madochee's mother was teaching him to steal and he would be killed if he was not taken off the streets.

Madochee is about 14 years old, at the writing of this book, and has always been able to fix most anything that was broken and could build rabbit cages, playhouses, and kites from almost nothing. He made the most masterfully and intricately designed kites that David and I have ever seen. His dad was hired as a guard at the Nutrition Center, keeping out older kids who were not in the nutrition center program and keeping peace among those who were. He tried hard to teach them to be thankful.

Chapter 13
Conflicted Schools of Thought

As more children were added to her home, Roberta continued to search for a better way to educate them. She was working with the poorest kids in Santo. She knew education was their only way out, but some of the leaders in their churches and in the Haitian school system beat them down psychologically. One preacher was heard saying, "Don't let any blanc (white person) tell you that you can move out of your station in life." Another person in the congregation broke the spirit of her son, David, by treating him as a second-class citizen, telling him repeatedly he couldn't rise above his station in life.

Haitian children have few, if any, rights or respect. A prime example of this is in the Haitian classroom. They live in fear of giving a wrong answer. Some of the students have no one to get them up and ready for school and they are especially vulnerable to embarrassment if his shirt is dirty or she came without a ribbon in her hair. Too often children are ridiculed by teachers and fellow students alike.

Children who fall behind in school must repeat a grade and have an added burden of being larger than others in his classroom. This stigma brings even more bullying and mistreatment. Lofane suffered daily because he was very tall for his age and because his family's poverty was extreme. He was made to hold rocks in the blazing sun with his arms outstretched and experienced beatings by the teacher many times.

Haitian schools teach by rote memory. It isn't important why 2+2=4, just that it does. If a student does not memorize well, he or she is at a severe disadvantage.

When a student learns information outside the classroom and tries to share it with the class, the teacher may feel threatened. Luckson (pronounced Luke-son), a young man from Cap Haiten, happened to visit Sonlight when Roberta and her children were studying astronomy. Roberta had a telescope and the class was looking at the universe. Instead of being amazed that Luckson had been able to use a telescope and had seen constellations and three planets, his teacher accused him of making up stories. The teacher, who incorporated voodoo and superstitions into his lessons on planets, declared Luckson could not have seen planets. Luckson was not given his full ten points and was shamed by his teacher in front of his classmates.

The most hideous injustice of all occurs when male teachers prey on pre-teen and teen girls, giving them a gift of new panties or lotion in exchange for "favors". Roberta overheard one teacher say to another, "I like the breasts when they've just begun to pop." It is understandable why girls sometimes don't want to go to school.

For all these reasons, Roberta wanted to homeschool her kids and to give the children a Christian education with a world view. She felt a strong need to change the destructive principles and integrate Christian ones. Even so, there were strong reservations from each side, Haitian and American. The Haitians didn't believe a child could rise above his circumstances and Americans didn't see the worth of an American education for a student who would live out his years in Haiti, a totally different culture.

But she forged ahead and tried various curriculums for a few years, none of which were satisfactory for the long term. She discovered Accelerated Christian Education (ACE) around 2007. Roberta was impressed and attended classes offered by ACE to learn how to best implement their curriculum. She knew it was exactly what she had been seeking. It took six months to get the school up and running. At first, all the children were excited --- until they realized you must work. They then thought it too hard and too slow.

Negativity began to raise its ugly head for two reasons. First, the children were bumping up against the idea of integrity: if you work hard, you learn; if you goof off, you get nowhere. Second, the older students did not understand the concept of participating and interacting with the teacher, such as raising your hand to ask "why" or "how" or to say, "I don't understand."

The Haitian way is to be silent until asked. Roberta's older children had been trained to sit, waiting for what the teacher might say or do next. Haitian children learn early they don't have responsibility in relationships --- perhaps because they are not regarded worthy? They never volunteered answers or made comments. It takes much perseverance and creativity to change the children's mentality of being non-participants.

The little children, on the other hand, loved the science projects and book reports and interacted with Roberta; they knew nothing else.

The curriculum was fulfilling for the self-starter student. Each student worked at his own pace using 12 workbooks for each class subject. When a student completed all 12 books of the ninth-grade math, he could then proceed to the next 12 workbooks of 10th grade math and so on. When all workbooks in each subject matter were finished, the pupil was ready to graduate from high school. With Michemana and Mack, this curriculum worked very well. They were self-motivated and eager learners. Michemana graduated with an exciting ceremony. Mack is still trying to finish his high school work.

Michmanna's Graduation Photo

However, the curriculum seemed to be ill-suited for students needing to be motivated and encouraged, which was most of Roberta's students. Eluide (pronounced Elweed), was the stabilizer, quietly trying to help the children stay on task. She is a gentle soul and well-loved by the children. Eluide graded papers for the children, but because her English is limited, she could not explain a math problem or how to conjugate a verb. Roberta was a great teacher but taking care of urgent business or crises pulled her away from the classroom much too often.

Roberta said she had no regrets about homeschooling --- she saved her girls from being raped and her boys would earn wages because they could speak and read English.

118

Kerlange Bathing Joseph

Roberta

Franky & Mack Game Night

Front Row: Macken; 2nd Row: Jo-Jo, Zach
Back Row: Mike, Luke, Joseph, Daniel, Micah

Kerline Offering Milk

Fresh Veggies from the Garden
Joseph, Mike, Micah, Daniel

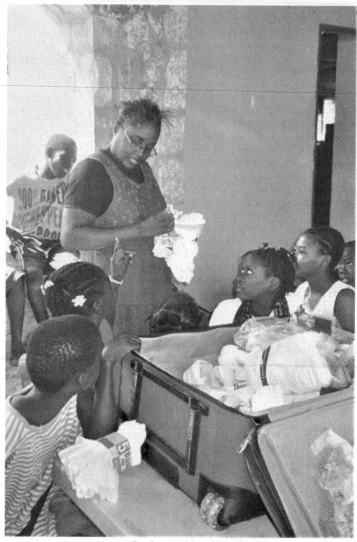

New Socks and Underwear

Wash Day, Madochee

Brotherly Love, Daniel & Mike

Roberta

Thankful Hearts
Shelda,Mirland,Michemana, Guerline

Enjoying a Meal with Megan McIntyre (front left) Courtyard
at the Guest House

PART IV
Taking a Peek into Roberta's Everyday Life

"Routine ruins the life, variety vitalizes the life."

Amit Kalantri, Wealth of Words

Chapter 14
Day by Day

On any given day in the life of Roberta and the children, you would have enjoyed sitting on one of the metal folding chairs in a corner of her living room, watching as the household awakened in the early morning hours. As sweet docility transformed into energy, all the chaos, chatter, and antics that followed throughout the day would have exhausted you. Then, when the sun fell behind the mountains and the children's tummies were full of supper, you, also, might have become drowsy as silence filled the house when the last child gave in to sleep.

At 5:30 a.m. some of the older children lumbered in with sleepy eyes and brooms made of banana leaves. My first visit after the family moved into the new house found me and my friend, Sandy, sleeping in the middle of the living room due to limited space. We were gently awakened with the swishing of brooms softly sweeping the floors. I felt like a spoiled American as they quietly worked, trying not to disturb our sleep.

When early morning chores were finished, breakfast was cooked, and the little children were dressed for the day, everyone gathered in the living room for the usual morning devotional. The next chapter of Proverbs was read by one of the children, comments were shared by the family, and a prayer closed the devotional. Breakfast was served. Breakfast options included cornmeal mush (seasoned with garlic, onion, and bell peppers), spaghetti noodles, oatmeal, or eggs.

Roberta

School was next. Early on, study cubicles were built for the older kids in the living and dining room areas, but they crowded out much-needed family space. A few years later, Roberta and the kids built a schoolroom on top of the little guest house out back --- remember a similar project she undertook back in the States while on her three-month sabbatical between jobs? Moving the school into the new addition was a great way to separate family life from school hours, but the schoolroom proved to be unbearably hot.

Roberta Teaching the Kindergartners

School was then moved to the side yard under the shade of the coconut trees for the little ones and to long tables under the carport for the older ones. Eluide supervised the older children and Roberta vacillated between teaching the kindergarteners and tutoring the older students. Melissa Maach, a graduate of Freed-Hardeman University, came for several summer internships and Laura Purvis, a member of the Estes church, came for several weeks at a time, both to help with the kindergartners. They were huge assets and encouragers for Roberta.

Franky and Judith Bringing Bread

School was over at noon for the smaller children and lunch was served. Noon-time meals were usually rice and beans topped with a tomato-based seasoned sauce containing vegetables such as bell peppers, onions, eggplant, carrots, okra, or cabbage, the same food served to the Nutrition Center children. Peanut butter on delicious Haitian bread was served as an alternative some days. After the older children finished lunch, they continued class until 2:00 p.m.

When school was finished, the bigger children worked at their various tasks of caring for the chickens, the rabbits, the fish, laundry, yard work, etc. The little ones played in the dirt, chased each other around the house, and squealed. Roberta oftentimes took a neighbor or church member to the doctor, sat at the Embassy trying to get a visa for one of the kids, conducted a Bible study, or held counseling sessions in her yard under the Plumeria tree.

When the sun's intense heat began to dissipate in the late afternoon, a couple of the older children began preparations for the evening meal. Rice and beans may have been served again, but perhaps dried fish or chicken would be included for added nutrition and variety.

Following supper, the children circled up as they gathered for the evening devotional in the house, under the carport, or out under the covered pavilion in the second yard. Mosquito spray was passed around as the singing started, anticipating a short Bible lesson prepared by one of the older boys. After questions were answered and discussed, prayer requests were given before the devotional closed with a prayer.

These devotionals are some of my sweetest memories with Roberta's family. The children loved to sing, and Roberta taught them the newest songs she learned on her latest visit to the Estes church. They sang enthusiastically and beautifully.

The sun would often just be going down and it felt delicious to have the gentle breeze blow through my wet hair, cooling it in the process. The tiredness from the day slowly seeped from my body as I felt completely relaxed, joyful, and contented as we worshipped.

We lost some of the little ones as their exhausted bodies gave in to sleep and slumped over their neighbor's lap. They were gently carried inside and taken to bed by bigger brothers and sisters. Before heading to bed themselves, the older guys oftentimes watched a football game (soccer) on TV while the girls shared hair style ideas and chatted. Before long, the house went quiet for the night.

Yet, if there was electricity or batteries, one corner of the house would most likely glow with the light of a computer as Roberta answered emails too numerous to count, figured out how to pay a bill, or maybe even read a chapter in her latest book, if she could stay awake. Early morning hours were reserved for her Bible reading, deep thinking, and prayer.

Such was a typical day at the Sonlight Children's Home. Many days ran amuck, especially when medical or VBS teams arrived, but these times of interruption were balanced out by experiences and relationships the children would not have had otherwise.

At one time, the kitchen wall held a chart with assigned rotating chores and somewhere else there were a set of written "rules of the house", all indicators that Roberta wanted the children to clearly know what was expected. Though she expected a lot from the children, she also had lots of fun with them as she introduced them to new experiences, foods, and knowledge.

Probably her very favorite outing with the children was taking them to the beach for the day. Though much of the ocean water on the shores of Haiti is polluted, clean water can be found after a couple of hours' travel time in a hot truck. The sweaty children frolicked and laughed as they enjoyed the coolness of the water, the older ones playing with and splashing the younger ones. Roberta packed sandwiches and Kool-Aid for lunch.

On one of our visits to Haiti, David and I went with the family to the National Museum of Haiti. It was sobering to see the history of Haiti in display --- pictures and statues of ruthless leaders and sculptures of enslaved men in chains were disturbing.

Though all Roberta's children were neatly dressed and well-behaved, it hurt my heart when the officials at the museum denied them access to the inside public bathroom, sending them outside instead.

Still another outing found us traveling up the mountain past Petionville to a small zoo operated by a Baptist organization. Though the animals were few, they were in natural-type habitats and well cared for. The children delighted at the colorful peacock, the scary tiger, and the silly monkey. It was cool atop the mountain with lots of shade trees and breezes, giving us a welcomed reprieve from the heat and humidity. We enjoyed lunch in the little café and, again, the children were all gentlemen and ladies.

Taking a group of 20 to 25 small children and teenagers anywhere can be a bit dicey, but there were never any real behavioral issues with Roberta's children. David and I always enjoyed the outings with these children who had happy countenances and expectations of a good time. Roberta was never wary of taking them out in public, but instead was proud to do so.

Our few trips to Domino's Pizza were no exception. We all liked to go to Domino's --- it was air-conditioned, clean, enough tables to sit us all, and they had good pizza (maybe the only pizza!). Sometimes a visitor to Sonlight would surprise Roberta with an invitation to take everyone out for pizza, giving Roberta and the older kids a much-needed break from the kitchen. We'd load up the Kia with the big kids filling up the truck bed while the rest of us squeezed into the large cab. Because of consistently heavy, slow traffic, it took us about two hours to make an otherwise 45-minute trip. With full tummies, the little children would sleep on the way home. How they slept while being thrown against each other as the truck wheels fell in first one pothole and then another, I don't know, but sleep they did.

Birthdays were always a big deal. Presents were not given, but Roberta had the honoree pick out his or her birthday meal and birthday dessert. I remember one night when the lights went out during our devotional, the little children began singing, "Happy Birthday to you". They thought Roberta was coming in with a birthday cake. It was their custom to shut off all the lights so the birthday candles would shine brightly.

As you may remember from her growing-up years, Roberta loved playing sports. Memorial funds in memory of Bob DeVall were used to pour a small basketball court with one hoop.

After a few years, she and the boys, with help from visitors, poured a full basketball court with basketball hoops on each end. Almost every evening Roberta dearly loved playing basketball with her boys while the girls chatted and giggled on the sidelines. The girls were welcomed to play, but rarely were they interested.

Roberta thought basketball was an invaluable tool in teaching the young men how to become a good team member. She even organized a community basketball tournament which was well-attended by the young people of the community. After two games, the tournament was cancelled due to neighborhood troublemakers, disappointing everyone.

Roberta Enjoyed Basketball

Roberta

The older she became, Roberta's abused knees began to yell at her. Consequently, her time on the court dwindled significantly, though hardly a week went by that she didn't get out there and try for a few minutes.

Friday nights were special times --- pizza-and-a-movie night! Roberta made all the crust and pizza sauce from scratch and taught her children how to make it. Pierre thoroughly mastered her techniques. You can imagine how much pizza it took to feed that gang, making her kitchen look and smell like a regular pizzeria.

Roberta would also pop a gigantic pan of popcorn to go with the latest DVD she brought from the States. Veggie Tales, westerns, and superheroes were favorites among the children. 20 minutes into a movie, you could hear Roberta softly snoring in a corner somewhere.

As part of trying to provide a well-rounded education, Roberta included the culinary arts. They tasted dishes from various countries such as Mexico, Italy, China (their favorite), and America, and heard a brief report of that country by one of the children.

To help with this and to provide more meat in their diet, David and I brought in 100 pounds of meat each time we visited. We could do this because of the generosity of two Churches of Christ in Eagan, MN, and Fulton, KY, as well as family and friends. We bought meats such as pork and beef roasts, ground beef, bacon, Italian sausage, chicken breasts, and two-pound blocks of mozzarella cheese for pizza-making. We re-packaged the meat into Ziploc bags, froze it for several days before departure, and then packed it tightly in coolers for the trip. When we arrived in Haiti 12 hours later, it was still frozen or partially frozen. Delays on one trip caused us to arrive 24 hours later; amazingly all the meat was still cold.

Remember the "mad cow disease" scare in early 2000? Although the US government confirmed only four cases in nine years, the Haitian security at the airport confiscated all the beef we brought in on one of our 2005 trips. That's the only time they've ever questioned our bringing in frozen meat. It made me wonder if somebody hosted a big barbeque that night in Port-au-Prince.

As always there was jubilant dancing and giggling as we loaded meat into the freezer at Sonlight. They knew good eating was coming. Roberta was an excellent steward of the meat, portioning it out and stretching it to last. The kids came to know and love such dishes as meatloaf, stews, lasagna, Chinese stir-fry, and of course, pizza. One night when pizza was served, I looked around and saw one of the children eating leftover beans and rice. Even though they have this meal daily, and sometimes twice a day, it is interesting to me how some still prefer it.

Chapter 15
God Moments

When asked to share with me her God moments, Roberta said there were too many to count. In exciting and unsuspected ways during her lifetime, God rescued her, making His presence felt. He filled Roberta with reminders that He is in control and He was taking care of her, even as she was keenly aware of kidnappers and the evil that abounds in Haiti. She carried a loaded gun in her purse the last weeks of her life.

But she rested in God's promises that He was with her, would strengthen and uphold her in His righteous hand, and would never leave her. (Isaiah 41:10, Deuteronomy 31:6).

She believed and lived the Scripture which says, "For if we live, we live for the Lord; if we die, we die for the Lord. Therefore, whether we live or die, we are the Lord's." (Romans 14:8).

These are a few of the stories Roberta shared with me, telling of God's rescues of her through the years:

--- The well on her property was one of only a few which held clean water. She called it God's well and allowed people to come into her yard and freely take water, though the custom was to charge for clean water. Three days in a row a man came, looked around, got his water, and left.

Early on a Sunday morning, someone knocked on her gate and frantically said they shouldn't go to worship because there was something bad to see at the right of her gate. Roberta and the kids went anyway, not looking toward the right. The man who came for water was lying dead by their gate. As it turned out, he was a thief and men from another part of town found and killed him.

... A voodoo priest had lived in the little house on their new property and horrible things had taken place in it. Having been asked to leave by the previous owners, he retaliated by casting evil curses and burying bottles over the yard. He claimed the house was Satan's.

When Roberta and the kids moved in, again he insisted that he wanted to stay and live in the small house. Roberta told him that it now was a house of God. He retaliated even more, performing bad curses and had evil people climb the trees and come over the wall, calling them "spirits". The girls were crying with fright. Roberta comforted them by encouraging them not to cry but pray instead. After a neighbor came to tell her the man had died, it brought to her remembrance the passage in Psalm 37:35-37: "I have seen a wicked, violent man spreading himself like a luxuriant tree in its native soil. Then he passed away, and lo, he was no more; I sought for him, but he could not be found. Mark the blameless man and behold the upright; for the man of peace will have a posterity."

... On a Wednesday night, as Roberta and the children readied themselves for Bible study, the preacher's wife knocked on the door, teary-eyed and upset. Two kidnappers (recognized as such because they were strangers in the small neighborhood) had been at Roberta's gate, waiting for her to come out and go to church. Tap-tap motorcyclists (men who make a living using their motorcycles to provide public transportation) held the kidnappers at the gate until the police arrived.

... Another kidnapping threat occurred when she and her family were out in an open field. The neighbors warned them all to get back in their car; a kidnapper was lurking about. These were two of about nine times when the Santo community prevented her kidnapping because they kept an eye out for strangers, their way of protecting Roberta.

... One day during Aristide's civil war, she had gone to town and, per usual, was sitting in traffic that was at a standstill. Men were in the street holding big rocks, going down the row of cars throwing the rocks at car windows. They hit the windows of the car in front of her and the car behind her but skipped hers.

... Almost dusk one evening (before cell phones were invented), she was returning from Petionville by herself in the countryside with no cars around and her tire blew out. She had gathered big rocks to use to jack it up when five men, farmers with straw hats and machetes, walked up to her. She was frightened and her adrenaline flowed. They changed her tire. In the instant she turned to hand them twenty dollars, they were gone. She called them her angels.

... Our last story happened when she was still married to the preacher. His eight-year-old cousin had club feet and he and Roberta had taken her to the doctor to see if there was any hope of surgery for the little girl. Sadly, the window of opportunity to correct her feet had passed when she was three or four years old. As they headed back home from the doctor, they heard shots ring out and an armed man approached their window and peered in at the little girl. He told his comrades he couldn't shoot this car because there was an angel riding with them.

Chapter 16
Ever the Visionary

Roberta had creative juices, intellect, and skills --- she needed several lifetimes to accomplish all that her mind could envision. Though she was always tired, she had enough passion, curiosity, and determination to override exhaustion and push forward on a new project. Her brain was ever working to figure out better ways to inspire and help the women and children of Haiti.

Some might think that turning your back, so to speak, on all the advantages of America and moving to a poverty-stricken country would squelch your opportunities to "be the most you can be". Roberta thought exactly the opposite. Haiti was a great place to reclaim and draw from the skills she learned as a child and a young adult. She approached life in Haiti with a heart of love and insight, enabling her to see countless opportunities and hope for others when they were too beaten down to see hope for themselves. She was smart, optimistic, and a hard worker --- and rarely gave up.

Roberta's most successful business venture was her chicken farm. She grew in knowledge as she experienced false starts and unfortunate situations.

She and the boys built chicken coops, bought a hundred baby chicks, and then lost them all to the hot Haitian sun.

A visitor helped Roberta build two portable domes that housed about seventy-five chickens each. When the chickens had eaten all the grass in an area, the wire dome was simply picked up and moved to another green section of grass, leaving the droppings in the previous area to fertilize the earth for new growth. The simplicity and advantages of such a commonsense approach excited her.

Chicken Coop

The system worked great for a good long while and the chickens produced a huge amount of big, brown eggs. Roberta never had a lack of buyers --- the Guest House cooks and women seeking to resell on the streets ensured a brisk business and profits.

The Nutrition kids started stealing chickens. The door to the chicken coops was left open and the dogs went on a killing spree. The successful business was pretty much wiped out. At the time of her death, Roberta was considering starting over with the chickens.

The other successful venture was establishing a sewing business with ladies from the local churches, called The Dorcas Sisters of Haiti. Roberta helped jump-start the business by purchasing fabric for the ladies who then sewed

142

purses, aprons, and skirts from patterns designed by a woman living in the States.

I valiantly attempted to locate this selfless woman without success. But she must be acknowledged and undoubtedly will recognize herself. She made many trips to Haiti to instruct and encourage Roberta and the Haitian sisters in this exciting effort. When local shops and vendors were not responsive, she brought the purses to the States to market them.

At the startup of this new business, the Dorcas Sisters truly stepped out in faith as they sewed twenty or thirty purses without pay. The ladies demonstrated the depth of their respect and trust in Roberta, since it is unheard of for a Haitian to work and not be paid. That's cause for revenge.

Eventually these purses sold in the US, but it took weeks before the ladies could ultimately pay themselves. Once they began to make a profit, Roberta showed them how to manage their earnings: give to God, pay themselves, and use the remaining funds to purchase more fabric to make more purses.

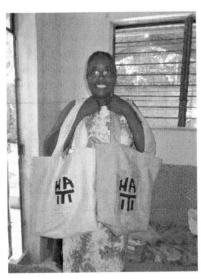

Proud Roberta with Purses

143

Roberta

Since Roberta's death, Sister Beaubrun has taken the lead on this work, but the women have struggled to find a way to get their business back on track without connections in the States.

The Dorcas Sisters of Haiti

In another business venture years ago, Roberta experimented with tilapia fish. Hearing about successes with tilapia fish farms, a group of us went to visit a farm. Before long, she and her boys had built about six concrete fish tanks, 5'x10' and smaller. Raising tilapia is a delicate and frustrating business and Roberta had moderate success for a time.

The earthquake damaged the tanks causing leakage, but also people just weren't buying. She lost money. Roberta continued to fight valiantly for three or four years, but eventually gave it up.

What do you do with empty fish tanks? 9-year-old Marie had an idea. David and I found her swimming in the murky, filthy, standing water one day. Knowing what her mom would say, she was terrified we would snitch on her. Marie pleaded her case, asking us to keep it our secret. We did.

Rabbits became an up and coming new business in Haiti and rabbit meat was beginning to sell in the elite grocery stores. Rabbit hutches were built at Sonlight, baby rabbits were bought, and soon they were grown and reproducing. But the average Haitian's palate was not yet ready for rabbit, it seemed, and sales were slow. The children in charge began slacking off and the old problem of stealing by the children in the Nutrition Center recurred. After a while, the rabbit business fizzled.

In yet another business venture, Roberta helped Eluide find a shop to rent and gathered an inventory of dresses to open a Wedding Shop --- I even sent her well-cared-for gowns from thrift stores here in Minnesota. Roberta was to be the silent partner while Eluide did the marketing and managing of the dress shop. The shop is still open, but Eluide's quiet personality makes it difficult for her to market her business alone.

Roberta was always on the alert for business ventures that could become livelihoods for her children and for the women of Haiti. Other ideas she entertained were opening a bakery, a catering service, and a resort in beautiful Jeremie. Selling small packets of drinking water on the streets is a lucrative business, but the government's many regulations and required paperwork shut down that idea almost as soon as it was formed.

PART V
A World Turned Upside Down

"And there was a trembling in the camp, in the field, and among all the people. Even the garrison and the raiders trembled, and the earth quaked so that it became a great trembling."

I Samuel 14:15

Chapter 17
A House Shouldn't Rock

Roberta was turning 50 years old on January 26, 2010. Her parents wanted to honor their daughter with a luxurious, pampering cruise that would loosen up every tight muscle in Roberta's tired body, giving her complete rest. Though this was not what Roberta would have chosen for herself, she, in turn, wanted to honor her parents by allowing them this gesture of their love.

So, when the earth began to shake and her house began to rock in Santo on Tuesday, January 12, 2010, Roberta was on a cruise ship, hundreds of miles away from her children.

While she scrambled to find a way to disembark the ship to reach her family, 23-year-old Thomas had a heavy responsibility land squarely on his young shoulders.

He was bathing the young children on the carport while Shelda was dressing the toddlers inside. They had never experienced a quake before, but Mom had taught them what to do and Thomas yelled for everyone to get out of the house. They grabbed the babies and the children ran to safety screaming, stumbling, panicked, and horrified.

Michemana remembered she was curling her hair as she felt her chair begin to shake. She ran, every step hard to take, as if the house were pulling at her, causing her to move from side to side. She was silent and stunned but followed her instinct to keep running as the house made loud rumbling noises. Pictures fell from the walls and bookshelves overturned. The concrete house swayed side to side. The security wall between Roberta's two properties collapsed. People were yelling everywhere and a cloud of dust rose into the sky.

After the shaking stopped, they counted heads and discovered one child missing, 15-year-old Nicky. They searched everywhere for him. Not finding him outside, they decided he must be trapped inside the house under furniture. Though afraid the house was unsafe, they were in panic mode and rushed back in, calling his name urgently. Silence.

They then remembered Nicky had been playing basketball by himself before the quake. They saw the fallen wall and knew where he must be. Blood on the broken wall left them sadly assured as to where Nicky lay. His body was badly crushed, but they took comfort in thinking his death must have been quick and probably he had not suffered.

The children started crying after finding Nicky; a heartbreaking time. Darkness was approaching and they were unable to retrieve his body. That gut-wrenching job had to wait until the next day.

Thirty minutes after the quake, Thomas' birth mom called him. After that, all communications went down. Aftershocks of the earthquake, less severe but still strong, continued every 20 to 30 minutes for the next day or two. Some were felt even a week later. Being afraid to go back in the house for bedding, the children retrieved clothes from the clothesline and spread them out on the concrete basketball court in the adjoining yard. To sleep on the concrete slab felt safer for two reasons: if another quake came, they thought it more solid than the ground and, also, there would be nothing above their heads to fall on them.

The children tried to sleep, but sleep was elusive. Not only were they in shock from the quake, but they felt vulnerable since the security walls had been breached during the earth's shaking. They knew people were going to become desperate and desperate people do desperate things, like stealing what is needed or wanted for survival, causing physical harm, if necessary. For protection, the children gathered rocks and placed them in a circle around themselves to use as weapons.

Feeling stunned and overwhelmed, Thomas asked himself, "What do I do next?" He was shaken and felt very small, but as the oldest, he knew the other 26 children were looking to him for leadership. Soon a large part of the community would also be looking to Thomas for guidance. He was in despair and afraid, yet he needed to figure out what to do.

When Wednesday morning dawned, Thomas checked the status of the generator and found he could start it right up. He sent a "way too short" e-mail to his mom: "Nicky died, walls down, rest of us safe". The next order of business was to reclaim Nicky's body.

As they were digging Nicky's body out of the rubble with pickaxes and shovels, many church members started arriving at their house, asking to stay. They headed to the one place where they had always found help --- Roberta's home.

Thomas was in a quandary. Saying "yes" invited additional financial issues with more mouths to feed and additional logistical issues concerning safety. He knew the reality of saying "yes" also meant he could no longer say "no" in the future. He wondered what decision his mom would make. Thomas said "yes," not knowing how in the world he was going to feed his family of 27, the 100 Nutrition Center children, and now the church members. But his young family was happy, because more trusted faces to sleep with meant more safety. There were a lot of people for supper Wednesday night.

Having retrieved Nicky's body, they realized they had a new problem --- no funeral home to call for the body. Most businesses had collapsed and the remaining funeral homes were overflowing with bodies. Thomas announced they would

151

need to bury Nicky themselves. A wooden box was made and, with the help of church members, a gravesite was prepared.

As the grave was being dug, thoughts turned to needed food and supplies. Funds were especially tight at the Sonlight Children's Home before the earthquake and they did not have an abundance of food. Roberta had left emergency money with Thomas in case of medical needs, but they were eating meagerly. God shows His care and love in mysterious ways --- often providing for us before we know we need it. Jesse Robertson and his mission team had just left Haiti the day before the earthquake and as he was leaving, he gave Thomas an envelope to give to his mom upon her return. Jesse had no clue how precious that money would become to Thomas.

Thomas and some of the older boys went to the streets in search of food and charcoal, the common fuel of choice. Navigating was difficult at best. Power lines were down, rubble and dead bodies everywhere, and thousands of people were walking the streets in shock, saying, "Oh, God." There were men in dump trucks collecting dead bodies like they were a pile of garbage --- dumping them and returning for more.

The boys found charcoal at double the price and continued to search for an open grocery. Several hours later they found one with lines out the front door. Finally making it inside, the boys discovered limited supplies of beans, rice, oil, and peanut butter, also at double the cost.

As they arrived back home, they found the grave had been dug. They buried Nicky next to Paul David.

During the night when he was alone, Thomas' tears came. He was comforted and strengthened by his brothers and sisters as they sought to help in any way Thomas needed them. Sylvio, David, and Francky helped repair fallen walls and traveled the streets in search of food. Shelda, Mirlande, Michemana, and Kerlange cooked food for their family and for all those who showed up in their yard during the days to come.

Joshua Wyatt arrived. Husband to Rachel Wyatt, Joshua is a preacher from the Millington Church of Christ near Memphis, TN, and long-time participant in the Estes-sponsored mission trips. Even though the Port-au-Prince airport was shut down and ground transportation was almost non-existent, Joshua took a leap of faith and set out to reach the children, trusting God to make a way for him. He flew into the Dominican Republic and from there took an unauthorized flight on an eight-seater prop-plane with a pilot who seemed to be accustomed to flying under the radar. Thomas was amazed when he saw Josh walk up.

After Joshua's arrival, Thomas held a small ceremony for Nicky. They invited members of the community to join them as they sang songs and prayed. Thomas spoke, continuing to shoulder responsibilities reserved for men beyond his years. He reminded the grieving children that God was still in control and, though we may not understand why, we must remember our ways are not His ways. The hurting hearts of the youngsters questioned how God could be in control if this could happen to Nicky; faith versus the reality of life.

Chapter 18
"Mom's Home!"

Roberta was desperately trying to make it back to Haiti, threatening to swim the Atlantic Ocean to get to her children. It was Saturday, after the earthquake on Tuesday, when she finally found a flight to the Dominican Republic, followed by a bus trip to Port-au-Prince. She told me that as she traveled past crumbled buildings and walked the debris-filled streets, she had the distinct feeling she was in an alien movie. The streets were crowded with people whose faces were blank and hollow with shock. Arriving home, she found a hundred people in her yard.

When told by Thomas they had enough food for one week, Roberta's response was, "Set aside two days for us and give the rest away. We have to start feeding people."

She had no way of knowing when or if more food would be forthcoming. This kind of faith and this kind of resolve was the reason God could use her to make a difference in the lives of so many people.

While trying to get home to her family, Roberta was on the phone with the Estes church leadership and Norm, formulating a game plan to get desperately needed food into the hands of Haitians. The earthquake left about 250,000 people dead, schools and government buildings in shambles, and 30,000 businesses and 188,000 homes destroyed. The earthquake left stunned, shocked, and dazed people who stumbled around as they tried to find their family members while stepping over bodies in the rubble-filled streets. Where do you go for help in a country that was pretty much at ground zero before the earthquake?

Foreign aid began pouring in, tent cities were created, and supplies arrived for thousands of grateful people.

God's people rallied and began sending funds and groups of people to provide physical labor. God, in His wisdom, had known what would be helpful in expediting emergency care to the people of Port au Prince --- a guest house for visiting medical and mission teams.

Previously, the medical teams stayed in expensive and inconvenient hotels. The Guest House was a much better hub from which the mission teams could work, located in Santo and just a short distance from the Sonlight Children's Home. This purchase brought comfort and reassurance to Roberta, further confirming that the Estes church was vested in this ministry and planned to stay, the Lord willing --- the same reassurance she felt when a house had been bought for her and the children.

The first team arrived in early January 2010 and returned home the day before the earthquake hit. As soon as transportation into Haiti was available after the quake, people came in groups and individually to serve in any way possible. The Guest House needed much work to make it truly livable. That first medical team and the following relief workers endured heat without fans, sometimes no running water or electricity, and ate whatever food snacks they brought with them. Jesse still talks today of the selfless and beautiful way these Christians labored and served.

The Estes medical mission teams now had the convenience of a gathering place and the proximity to Roberta's home was a blessing, saving time and effort that would otherwise been spent navigating crowded, bumpy roads.

The church collected and managed 2.4 million dollars given by over 24,000 donors. They sent in disaster relief teams to restore security, provide aid, and begin rebuilding. It was a blessing that neither the Sonlight Children's Home nor the Guest House was seriously damaged.

Because the overwhelming needs soon exhausted the church's personnel, Larry Waymire, a preacher from Lexington, TN, was recruited in 2010 to make regular trips to Haiti and direct the relief program. Rachel (who had spent a year with Roberta in Santo 15 years ago) and her husband, Jason Baker, joined the relief effort. They moved, with their two babies, to Haiti for short term, fulltime work at the Guest House. Tons of food were sent to Haiti over a two-year period and over a hundred homes were built. Many homes were repaired, six congregations received new places of worship, and new schools were established. Most importantly, many people were believing and being baptized.

It was no easy feat to channel those funds, food, and supplies. The game plan made by Roberta, Norm, and the Estes church sent food and water into the Dominican, along with tents, mosquito netting, and other supplies. Brother Jean Claubert loaned his Kia for the emergency. Roberta and one of her boys drove to the Dominican Republic/Haiti border to meet Norm and his crew. By the time Norm and his crew bought food and supplies, loaded the goods, and arrived at the border, it was nighttime. Nighttime hours were helpful: fewer people on the road meant enhanced protection from thieves.

Soon the big blue Daihatsu was purchased and 3,000-4,000 pounds could be transported per trip and with fewer security checks because the Daihatsu had Dominican Republic license plates. Roberta and one of her sons would drive the supplies home where the rest of the children helped unload, re-bag the 50-pound bags of rice and beans into smaller bags and distribute the food. Roberta and one of the boys would head back to the Dominican border the following night. These clandestine trips continued for over a month and then huge containers started arriving by sea. It would serve no purpose to discuss why containers of rice sat and soured in the port because it was not released to the people.

The Daihatsu

The lives of the children living at the Sonlight Children's Home were forever changed as their property became a distribution center. The Sonlight family worked unceasingly for about a month, sleeping only when their bodies could take no more. The children continued sleeping in tents out in the yard for four or five months following the earthquake, even though their mom slept in the house as soon as it was deemed safe. The continuous aftershocks screamed, "Unsafe!" to the children.

The pace slowed down after a month, but even so, for the next five to six months, they arose at 4:00 a.m. and worked until 11:00 p.m. Thomas tells of falling asleep behind the wheel one night and being awakened by the bumpy side of the road. They were all exhausted and the whole experience took a huge toll on the family. After five months, the initial intensity of the relief work eased, but relief work lasted another three years.

Learning the safest, most expedient way to distribute the food and supplies was an ongoing process and they never found a satisfactory system. Some were a little better than others, but all had their dangerous moments. Originally, Sonlight was used as a base of operations. After desperate people damaged their security gate and front wall and shoved Roberta's children, distribution from the home ceased.

They then tried using their truck. With Roberta behind the wheel and the teenage children in the truck bed, they went through the streets handing out bags without ever bringing the vehicle to a stop. The big drawback to this approach was people in the church were not getting food.

Yet another approach made use of the pavilion in their adjoining property, which was also protected by four walls and had two gates. They would allow a group of people inside, lock the gate behind them, give each a bag, and then let them exit through the second gate. This, too, had its anxious moments when a group of young men would not listen, got angry, and threatened to shoot the workers handing out food with guns they claimed to have in their pockets. Thankfully, the rest of the crowd helped control them and the moment passed.

Food reached the eager people. Realizing that Roberta and her family were constantly exhausted, the Estes church enlisted the help of Brother Jean Claubert Belton and other preachers around Port-au-Prince. Food was purchased by the truckload and then distributed through the churches, relieving Roberta's burden.

Giving a gift is a universal event, whether it is a life-saving gift of food in a third world country or a thoughtful gift of love in America. How it is received is also universal, with a sense of entitlement or gratefulness. It was a blessing to Roberta and her children when the food and supplies were received with upraised hands and a "Thank You, God". It made them feel a little less tired.

Roberta

While Roberta and her crew were working in their community, tent cities were being constructed for the homeless and for those afraid of returning to their homes. One of the reasons for such widespread destruction was the substandard concrete blocks used for building the high-rise apartments. The unsafe concrete blocks gave way causing a "pancaking" effect as one floor collapsed onto another, trapping and killing the people inside. People were afraid the remaining buildings would also collapse.

Roberta and the Tent City

The tent cities squeezed together thousands of people on a small tract of land. In these adverse conditions, a strange thing was happening in the streets and in the tent cities: people were pulling together. Instead of attacking one another, they began helping one another, offering what towels or sheets they might have and performing other acts of kindness.

However, it is inevitable when you have hordes of strangers living in a limited amount of space for an extended time, the worst will come out in people. Housing was being built as quickly as possible by the Estes church and by hundreds of other churches, businesses, and governments from all over the world, but it took about three years to complete. In the meantime, these tent cities, which brought short-term relief, became plagued by rapes, thievery, violence, disease, and oppression. The need to get people out of there became urgent.

Chapter 19
Tenacity and Grit

No one who experienced the Haiti Earthquake of 2010 was left unscathed. Roberta was hurting --- for her suffering family and community and for herself. But as I said early on in this book, Roberta was no quitter.

She had already given 13 years of her life, energy, and love to Haiti and she would go on to give another seven years. She did not grow calloused or indifferent. Instead, she determined to keep her family intact while finding innovative ways to help the women of Haiti. Roberta knew the only way out of poverty for Haitian women and children was education and an opportunity to start their own businesses. Above all else, she determined to be the salt and light to a people who needed to be rescued, because she, herself, had been rescued. In her weakness, He was strong.

"We are afflicted in every way, but not crushed; perplexed, but not despairing; persecuted, but not forsaken; struck down, but not destroyed; always carrying about in the body the dying of Jesus, so that the life of Jesus also may be manifested in our body." (II Corinthians 4:8-10)

The tenacity and pure grit with which Roberta worked following the quake came directly from this Scripture. During her suffering, she found her strength in the Lord of lords and

King of kings. God will not be defeated and His people are always victors.

Though I am confident there were times she questioned her body and mind's abilities to endure until Haiti and her family stabilized, she knew her mission: do what was required of her in the next moment.

Roberta's world literally came crashing down. The scent of death permeated the very air she breathed. Devastation was as far as her eye could see. The huge task of saving lives overcame the temptation to crawl into a fetal position and give up.

The family worked tirelessly for months. As life tried to return to normalcy, Roberta soon realized what had been normal for them would never be again. Post-quake work for the community continued even as Roberta needed to restore much needed order to her own home. Because she had been overwhelmed with the non-ending relief efforts, discipline had become lax.

Roberta could not discipline and correct the children while she worked 18-hour days for months. Compounding the issue, she was enduring the trauma of death and suffering of masses of people who surrounded her. There was not enough physical presence, not enough emotional strength, and certainly not enough energy to love and train up 27 children during this tragedy. After a while, some of the older children quit listening and obeying. They began stealing money and food, giving it to their friends. They would not be corrected.

The Sonlight family was in a state of crisis and fragility. News of changes in the US Embassy's immigration policies heaped more chaos onto the home. Because the devastating earthquake left behind even more orphans, the US Embassy began allowing more Haitian children to be taken out of country. Someone offered to assist Roberta in getting her and the children out of Haiti and to the States.

Roberta declined because she believed it was in the best interest of the children and of the nation of Haiti if the children remained in their country. It was her hope that as the children were raised to be followers of Jesus, they would become the light in this dark country. They would be able to teach their birth families and friends about God's amazing love and mercy. They would pattern Jesus' teachings to love and take care of each other. They would spread hope among those suffering in Haiti.

Many medical, VBS, and preacher teams arrived on Sonlight's doorstep through the years, forming a great love and respect for Americans by the children. In their eyes, Americans were kind, generous, and loving people. They believed all Americans were wealthy and life came easy for those living in the United States.

Roberta made the decision to tell her children about this offer and she also told them why she declined.

They did not take the news well. A major rebellion ensued against their mom because she had denied them the opportunity to live in the United States. This was the "straw that broke the camel's back". Having endured months of hard labor, little sleep, and few rewards, they perceived moving to the States as their reward and Mom had snatched it from them. In April, three months after the quake, five of the teens left home. In July, Thomas left, followed by two more, making a grand total of eight teenagers leaving Sonlight. Roberta sadly referred to this period as "The Exodus".

This added insult to injury for her, just coming out of the aftereffects of the earthquake. Roberta was hurt and disheartened, yet doggedly determined to stay in Haiti with the remaining children. Moving back to the States had never been a viable option for her and this time was no exception.

The good news was that because of their English education, some of the older children who left could now earn wages translating and working for other evangelical missions in the country.

Thomas, of all the children, was the most conflicted in what he should do. Even before the quake, he was having misgivings about the lack of progression in his homeschooling. He was now 23 years of age and others around his age, like Marchodson, were moving on with their education. He grew increasingly restless. Because he was the oldest, most dependable, and had a good work ethic, Roberta depended on him heavily. His schoolwork was always second place after any urgent task --- and there were always urgent tasks.

During the earthquake and its aftermath, there was just no time or energy for school, setting him even further behind. When the workday was only 18 hours long, Thomas would try to study in bed with a flashlight, but his study time was stolen by the culprit called sleep.

Roberta and Thomas, April 2015

He tried to talk with his mom. He explained his frustrations that his schoolwork was never a priority. He couldn't get a definitive answer from her for a study plan or exactly where he was on his path to graduation. Roberta didn't feel the same urgency as Thomas. It didn't matter so much when he would finish his education, but that he finish. The gap between them grew wider and by July 2010 he had a plan in place to head to the States, even without Roberta's blessing.

When he came back for his first visit after "the Exodus", Thomas was concerned about the household. Roberta seemed exhausted and the remaining children still were not doing their chores but, instead, were doing pretty much whatever they wanted. Before the earthquake, chores were rotated through the children and consequences given when a child slacked off. The house was kept to a certain level of cleanliness. Now things seemed to have gone from bad to worse: bathrooms smelled, floors were dirty, and the house was a mess.

Marchodson, the same young boy who tried to knock down mangos from trees to share with the other children, came to live and work with Roberta as he prepared to go to medical school in St. Kitts. He and Thomas attempted to do whatever jobs needed to be done to improve the condition of the house, but Roberta would respond with, "The kids need to do it." It was her new tactic, but the children wouldn't do it, so it never got done. It seemed she was overwhelmed and no longer had strength to be the disciplinarian.

Although she could never move back to the US and leave her children, Roberta began to rethink the feasibility of adopting the younger children and taking them to Tennessee. A large affordable house came on the market in Henderson, big enough to accommodate the 10 or 11 younger children. However, getting visas and passports became hurdles Roberta could not overcome and that dream died.

Chapter 20
Navigating Through
Turbulent Waters

Because Roberta never forgot to Whom she belonged, the earthquake and its aftermath did not destroy the driving force within her. She was weary, discouraged, and hurting, but she clung to Paul's words in II Corinthians 4 when he reminds us, "God's treasure is in earthen vessels so that the surpassing greatness of the power will be of God and not from ourselves" --- the powerful Gospel is in us, clay jars.   Roberta understood clearly she was a clay jar. God's power and His mercy guided her through these post-quake days, helping her navigate the turbulent waters of her life. She also knew whatever powerful and great thing came from this devastation would be from God. Roberta was counting on that.

With God on her side, she would not be defeated in her efforts to continue helping ease the burdens of people in physical and spiritual poverty. Roberta's mission for her children and the people of Haiti was to glimpse the goodness of God and His love for them, owning a new hope that only comes from the Father.

Roberta had no illusions about "saving Haiti". The political corruption, the stranglehold of voodoo, the lack of medical care, an inadequate school system, and rampant starvation are all sources of overwhelming discouragement to well-meaning souls who want to save Haiti. Her mission from the time she stepped onto Haitian soil was to help the person in front of her, just like Jesus did.

In August 2011, three-month-old Jonathan (also known as Jo-Jo) became the person in front of Roberta. Another baby for her bed.

His mother, a cousin of one of the local preachers, died during childbirth. When Jonathan arrived at Roberta's door, they did not expect him to live; he looked like an old man. He had no hair, sores on his scalp, and only weighed five pounds. The household began the same regimen as with the other suffering babies who came to live with them: '50 kisses, 100 hugs, and good milk. In three weeks, he was laughing.

Jonathan was one of those children who had a natural sensitivity --- he easily showed affection and expected nothing in return. He had an uncanny sense of when to go up and give Roberta a hug or bring her a flower or just come sit on her lap and be very still. His love-language was serving and it came from his heart. He liked to help wipe down the tables after a meal, wash dishes, sweep, or dig in the garden. He loved to play and fool around; knowing when to stop was his issue.

As Roberta helped one person at a time, she continued to use the same strategies in spiritual warfare she had always relied upon --- prayer, love, and a servant heart. She loved and taught her children. She prayed for long-range effects as they grew and shared Christ with their birth families and friends. For those living outside her home, she shared out of her bounty or out of her poverty, she prayed with them and for them, and she tried to open the doors of their hearts with Jesus' love.

In America, there are sections of our cities that are poverty-stricken. Most of us tend to avoid such areas; it's unpleasant and silently demands a response from us. The whole country of Haiti is one such area. Almost every person one encounters needs something urgently: food, clean water, clothes, shelter, or money. Everywhere Roberta walked or drove, people needed something from her. I grew ever impressed that she didn't seem to harden to their pleas, realizing she was but one person with limited resources. She was human and at times felt overwhelmed, helpless, and discouraged at all the unmet needs. It took strength and faith for her to do what she could, for as many as she could, for as long as she could, and leave the rest in God's hands and claim His peace.

Roberta continued to lay down her life daily. She cared for dying babies, oversaw the household chores and preparation of meals, had late-night talks with teenagers, and shared her bed with two or three little ones who needed the comfort of their mom more than she thought she needed a good night's rest.

Roberta figured out generator problems in the middle of the night because Americans sleeping on her property needed fans. She dealt with sewage backup in her house and yard; she cooked breakfast for 150 Nutrition Center children at 6:00 a.m. when the cook couldn't get there. Roberta transported people/groups from the airport while still planning, shopping, and executing their meals; picked up car parts for the latest vehicle up on blocks; and found somebody on the streets to repair a tire once again eaten up by road debris. While she was doing these things, her children saw her not giving up.

She continued to give away rice and beans at her gate. Roberta gave a listening ear daily to broken-hearted moms, distraught and desperate people looking for ways to survive. She taught her children to love and serve as they climbed into the back of her truck to take food to an AIDS patient or to a 15-year-old single mom or a cake to celebrate a birthday.

A preacher in Mexico, with a wife and six children contracted a fatal disease and was in serious financial difficulty. The children at Sonlight, on their own, took up a collection of their earnings from translating at the clinics and their birthday monies to send to the family. Roberta's examples of selflessness were being mirrored by her children. She

171

understood that it was not just making it through each day with her children that counted, but rather showing them the joy of looking beyond themselves, searching for what they could give or give up, lightening another's burden.

Roberta was a saint, as are all God's children, but she was not perfect. She sacrificed herself daily for many years, but she lost her temper, gave out punishments unbefitting the crime, didn't always make wise choices, and she hurt people. Roberta knew she, like us, was one beggar telling another beggar where to find food. She knew she was made of clay and had no illusions to the contrary.

PART VI
The Gathering Place

"Let love of the brethren continue. Do not neglect to show hospitality to strangers, for by this some have entertained angels without knowing it." (Hebrews 13:1)

Chapter 21
Clinics, Bunk Beds, and Food

When Roberta's marriage fell apart, God put people in her life who held up her arms and encouraged her, assuring her she was not alone in her resolve to continue her ministry in the Port-au-Prince area. She was blessed with a large, beautiful house and Christians to rally around and encourage her.

Now, after this second catastrophic event, again God provided just what Roberta needed, exactly when she needed it. And though guests at the Guest House meant added work for Roberta, they also brought her companionship and laughter as they labored together. Roberta was never to feel as alone again in Haiti as she had felt that first year after her divorce.

Before the earthquake, most medical teams were sent by the Estes church. Later, their sister congregation, the Henderson Church of Christ, also began sending down an annual team.

Since the acquisition of the Guest House, medical mission team leaders have slowly developed a system that both satisfies and expedites their needs while in Haiti. A handy man is included on the team to work on the never-ending repairs and improvements for the Guest House and at the Sonlight house.

Roberta

Jesse Robertson and Roberta

Jesse has led these teams for 27 years. He organizes transportation to and from Haiti, creates the schedule, finds and coordinates team members, and has honed all the components like a well-oiled machine. Jesse's adult son and daughter, Jacob and Emily, have accompanied him on some of the trips while his wife, Kayla, stayed behind with their youngest daughter, Anna.

Jan Sharp coordinates food for the teams going down. She cooks, freezes, and ultimately packs the food for the journey to Haiti. In addition, Jan spends months collecting adult/children clothes, shoes, diapers/baby clothes for baby bags, linens, canned goods, fabric, sewing machines, medicines, etc., turning her garage into a small warehouse. In years gone by, the airlines allowed two checked bags per traveler and a carry-on. The carry-on was claimed by the traveler, while Jan filled every inch of the 72 checked suitcases for the 36-member mission team. New luggage policies have cramped Jan's style.

These campaign trips have become an annual family affair for the Sharp family. Jan's husband, Roy, has served as an elder in both the Estes and the Henderson churches and travels with her on each trip. They are accompanied by their daughter, Rachel Wyatt, and her husband, Joshua, along with three of their grandchildren: Cora, Florine, and Cyrus. For years, the Sharps' house was Roberta's home when visiting in Henderson.

Jan and Roy Sharp

The medical part of the team is led by nurse practitioner, Scott Miskelly. His wife, Kristy, and their children, Darby, Wilson, and Madelyn, travel with him as part of the mission team. For more than five years, the family has been on a quest to adopt two little Haitian boys, Cherdinor and Davidson. Government paperwork and politics have been horrendous, but they are hopeful to bring them home soon.

Roberta

Scott Miskelly in Clinic

Doctors and nurses, along with the optometrist and a pharmacist, Jeanne Evans, accompany Scott. Jeanne comes a week prior to the team, organizing and re-packaging medicines for clinics in the upcoming week.

Though others have also repeatedly been members of these medical teams, Jesse, Jan, and Scott are the tireless souls who have served as organizers for about fifteen years and plan to continue for as long as God can use them. They made their first trip back to Haiti after Roberta's death in June 2017 and a second one last year in 2018. A planned trip in May of this year, 2019, was cancelled due to the dangers of political unrest in Port au Prince.

The rest of the 36-plus team members are made up of people who come to register patients and direct traffic, assist with exams, entertain children, pass out medicines, and teach Bible classes to waiting patients. Because Henderson, TN, was Roberta's home base when she returned to the States, all these team members were friends of hers who had become like family. The week was like a working family reunion, of sorts, and though she was physically exhausted from the

178

workload, she was spiritually and emotionally energized by their presence.

As the medical team prepared for their trips, their constituency in the Caribbean Sea was also preparing with much anticipation. Roberta laid the groundwork needed to prepare the churches in Santo and neighboring towns for the team's visit. She informed each preacher of his clinic date, asking him to notify and organize the church members. She ensured there were enough tables, chairs, and tarps ready to be transformed into clinic stations --- and hunted down all the large water coolers the team used last year!

Translators mainly were her children, but often more were needed and Roberta sought out and hired qualified young people living outside her home. One of her tougher jobs was making sure there were enough available, operational vehicles to transport 50 people. All the while, Roberta was still mother to 20+ children, a fulltime job itself.

Roberta and Se Marie, a Haitian woman and long-time friend of Roberta's, planned and organized Haitian suppers to supplement Jan's American meals. Se Marie provided clean linens for the beds and bathrooms and tried to rid the bunk beds of their ever-present coating of dust.

Roberta bought fresh fruits and vegetables for the week and made sure the kitchen and pantry were well stocked, including cold soft drinks in the beverage 'fridge.

Ricardo, the Guest House caretaker, and his three-year-old daughter, Rosie, lived in a tiny house on the property. He was responsible for opening and closing the gate, maintaining and operating the large generator, keeping the yard tidy, and the endless tasks of sweeping and mopping floors.

Ready or not, the big day arrives! The team has been up since 2:00 a.m., lugging massive amounts of luggage and running for airplanes. Though physically tired, they are hyped about being back in Haiti and anticipating the work they will get done while there. Bunks are claimed, luggage stowed, and supper is eaten. After regrouping for the next day's activities and schedule, they all get still for a quiet devotional --- then race each other to one of the two indoor bathrooms.

The sleepy-eyed team begins its day like it ended the day before --- taking turns in the bathrooms. They then head to the kitchen area for breakfast of perhaps Haitian oatmeal, or bacon and eggs, or bagels and cream cheese, or maybe some homemade scones.

Soon tables, chairs, and tarps are loaded onto the big truck. Rachel brings along her tools needed to perform eye exams --- in a few weeks, glasses will be sent back to the patients.

Rachel Wyatt

Hundreds of children's vitamins, Tylenol, antibiotic ointment, blood pressure medicine, and worm pills are some of the typical medicines given out to 300-500 patients each day and have been safely stowed away in the truck. Lastly, sandwich makings for lunch and large coolers of water are hoisted onto the truck before they depart around 7:30 a.m., headed for one of the local church properties.

A Clay Jar Too Soon Broken

Estes Church Medical Mission Team
Headed out for Their Clinic

Open sores, machete wounds, cysts, and fevers are the more common conditions that bring patients to the clinic, but people with an extra finger on the hand or with webbed fingers have received minor surgeries. One man presented himself with a bullet that had been embedded for seven years in his leg bone.

Patients Waiting to Enter Clinic

Roberta was needed at the clinics to translate and help with medical emergencies or other serious situations.

Roberta

One of the scariest moments the team experienced was in trying to save tiny Micah's life. If you will remember, he was lactose intolerant, had malaria, and was experiencing projectile vomiting. Starving Micah gulped down several combinations of formula created for him, only to explosively throw it up. A shot of rocephin was given in his "skinny butt" and eventually his lungs began to clear. One of the skilled nurses, Tracy, finally got an IV in his little arm that would deliver the life-saving fluids and malaria meds. Roberta and Jan frantically roamed the streets seeking a formula that was milk-based but without lactose and finally found it. He kept the milk down and began to gain weight.

Last Minute Instructions

After laboring in the heat all day, the sweaty, exhausted team returned to the Guest House between 6:00-7:30 p.m., where a hot meal and cold showers awaited them. There was lots of bantering and jesting going on about this time, releasing the heaviness of what the group had experienced at the clinic.

Roberta went home to her children but returned to the Guest House after supper to be spiritually fed by a devotional of beautiful songs, meaningful thoughts, and prayer before they packaged pills for the next day and went to bed. When living in a foreign country, it's like a soothing ointment to sing songs of praise in your native tongue with a group of people who love you dearly.

Bunk beds feel wonderful at the end of the day and the group is grateful for the many fans that stir the hot, sticky air, making it a bit more difficult for mosquitoes to bite.

Roberta and Roy Sharp
Lollipops Make Everything Better

Chapter 22
Serving the Servants

David and I have traveled off and on to Haiti for 24 years. The last 14 years were spent working with Roberta, our friendship growing ever deeper. We still had two teenagers living at home, so we often took turns making our trips.

David loaded his coolers with frozen meat and made a trip every three months for two years to hold seminars. Roberta was eager for the young preachers and churches to hear God's Word preached by a seasoned speaker. A seminar was an all-day preaching event held on a Saturday, with rice and beans prepared and served by Roberta and her girls at the noon break. David also preached Sunday morning and taught the adult Bible class, with Thomas usually translating.

After a while, David enlisted help from family and friends to travel with him and speak at the seminars: his brother, Cecil May, Jr.; our son, Michael May; our preacher in Minnesota, Tommy Carr; and the preacher at the Palm Beach Lakes Church of Christ in Florida, Dan Jenkins.

My trips were to encourage Roberta. I like to think I was helping to hold up her arms. I loaded my bags up with frozen meat, chocolate chips, 2-pound blocks of mozzarella cheese, games to play with the children, brightly colored ribbons for the girls' hair, and deflated basketball and soccer balls for the boys. As Roberta vented, I listened and listened and listened. On some of my trips, Roberta would organize a Ladies' Day at one of the local churches. I taught while one of Roberta's girls translated and craft materials were brought for the ladies to make take-home gifts. My second job was to spoil my second set of grandchildren.

In 2012, our personal funds which supported our "Haiti Habit" were about exhausted. Since we were empty nesters for the first time, we decided to downsize from our house to a condominium to help with cash flow.

Shortly after putting our house on the market, we traveled down to Haiti. We took Roberta to lunch and while enjoying our meal outside with a lovely tropical breeze cooling us, Jesse telephoned Roberta. After a brief conversation, she said, "I don't know – why don't you ask them?" David's eyes widened as he heard Jesse ask him if we would be interested in hosting the Guest House.

After the initial "deer in the headlights" reaction, we began to think what a great opportunity this would be. Offering fresh beds, hot meals, and cool drinks to weary servants coming to labor in Haiti sounded very appealing. Living around the corner from Roberta and our second set of grandkids made it even more appealing. But at our ages, 69 and 70 years old, were we physically up to the challenge? We were excited, but scared.

Our thoughts then turned to concern for our family. One of our sons lives in Tampa, FL, but our other four children, their spouses, and our six grandchildren lived only 10 to 45 minutes from our house in Minnesota. In a very real way, we are the only parents and grandparents our married children and their spouses have and gaps would be left upon our departure. Few parents get to live in such proximity to their children and grandchildren. Who goes off and leaves them behind?

We prayed and pondered and prayed and pondered, asking for wisdom. All our children gave us their blessings --- some more guarded than others. The elders at Estes were thoughtful and generous in offering transportation and time for us to spend with our children.

As for our health and energy concerns, there are a lot of "what if's" in this life to keep us paralyzed. We had confidence God would equip us with what we needed for His work. Ultimately, we felt compelled to say "yes", and in August 2012, we moved to Haiti. It has been one of the more enriching parts of our lives. Our health allowed us two years in Haiti before we were forced home to be near our doctors.

God's timing is always perfect. We marveled how, at just the opportune moment, He orchestrated all the variables to provide hosts for the Guest House, funds for our continued travel to Haiti, and a bonus --- to live and work alongside Roberta.

God kept His promise "to do far more abundantly beyond all that we can ask or imagine, according to the power that works within us." (Ephesians 3:20). He is awesome!

Roberta met us at the airport with her huge smile and open arms and brought a couple of her boys to relieve us of massive luggage. We bounced and jostled, laughed and talked all the way to the Guest House in anticipation of the great days ahead.

Ricardo opened the gates wide at the honk of our car and he and Se Marie greeted us with smiles and a hot Haitian supper. But the first thing to be done was to get Roberta's meat separated out and delivered over to her house, where we would be overrun with hugs and greetings from the children. We felt blessed to have two places in this world where we felt needed, welcomed, and loved.

Roberta

David & Charlene at Guest House

As David and I settled in at the Guest House, Se Marie and Ricardo helped us sort out the clutter and rubbish left by earlier mission teams. We organized the useful items and deep cleaned as we went. Haiti is synonymous with "dust bowl". You can dust a shelf in the morning and write your name on the same shelf in the afternoon. Because no one had been managing the Guest House for months, there were layers upon layers of dust and grit.

Once the clutter was cleared out, Se Marie and I attacked the bare-bones kitchen, emptying and scrubbing all the shelves in the food pantry, the dish pantry, and the bins holding kitchen supplies. We set out rat traps and ant poisoning.

A Clay Jar Too Soon Broken

Se Marie   Ricardo & Rosie

Knowing of the sparseness of supplies, I had been given an allowance and brought in a couple of suitcases filled with kitchen tools, durable plastic glasses, plates, tablecloths, etc. I cooked without an oven for the first two months until a lovely stove with an oven was installed in an adjacent work room. That was Roberta's suggestion to keep the kitchen a bit cooler.

Even though Roberta no longer had to oversee the physical care of the Guest House, she was still my consultant and go-to person. We especially needed her to explain Haitian culture and customs, so we would embarrass ourselves and our staff as little as possible. Roberta got more than one desperate phone call from me.

After a few months, Se Marie left and Amancee was hired to cook our Haitian meals, supplementing my American meals for the guests. She also prepared the Guest House for their arrival and cleaned up after their departure, washing mounds and mounds of sheets and towels left behind by the huge groups.

Roberta

Though we had an electric washing machine, it was archaic and temperamental. It held two compartments and clothes had to be transferred from the washing side to the spinner side. The spinner side oftentimes did not operate properly and Amancee spent hours wringing sheets and towels by hand, hanging them out to dry.

A second washing machine was purchased to speed along the process, but it seemed one of the two machines was always broken. After a big group, it could take a week for Amancee to get all the clean linens back into their plastic bins, stored there to protect them from Haiti's dust.

Amancee & Ronaldo

Ronaldo, who had eaten in the Nutrition Center as a child, was a young man Roberta recognized as having integrity and great potential. When Ricardo left the Guest House, Roberta hired Ronaldo and he has proven himself to be indispensable because of his strong work ethic, dependability, self-motivation, honesty, and most importantly his godliness.

Roberta would be proud Ronaldo has not only continued his good work ethic, but he is trying to finish high school and is enrolled in a mechanics' school.

Early each morning around 6:00, I heard the swish of his broom and smelled the disinfectant from his mop water as he attempted to keep the floors clean and dust-free, repeating the process in the afternoon. Ronaldo performed the same tasks as Ricardo, but he also cared for Jessica and Francesca.

Jessica and Francesca are two dogs descended from Sheba, the Rottweiler dog Roberta eventually brought to Haiti. Sheba turned out to be an excellent watch dog and bodyguard for Roberta. Sheba was gentle with the children and visitors, but if she sensed there was danger for Roberta, you best not get between them.

Dogs in Haiti are pitifully little and skinny. Jessica and Francesca are a formidable sight. When the gates open at the Guest House, people walking down the streets immediately stop and back up. Just knowing these big dogs live there is a security boost. One day, Roberta and I were putting together a wish list for the next large container being shipped in by Healing Hands International. Because she felt awkward asking for dog food and kitty litter, I suggested she mention these are needed for our security guards and our rat exterminator; she felt validated.

David and Ronaldo made a good team, working together to keep the mechanics of the property and house running smoothly.

Communication with Ronaldo and Amancee was a challenge --- Amancee spoke no English and Ronaldo's was limited. For a while, David set up daily English/Creole classes which benefited us all. Life got in the way and the classes eventually ended. But not all was lost --- I managed to teach Amancee how to say peanut butter, valuable because she asked daily to use it with her bread at lunch.

Roberta

The internet system was sketchy at best --- keeping it up and running could have been a fulltime job for David. He was greatly appreciated by all of us, including Roberta, since she had severely limited electricity at home. It was our life-link to our family and the outside world.

David also managed the financial books, was an excellent trouble-shooter for the many things that could and did go wrong in the course of a day, and was a visionary of how the property and operation of the Guest House could be improved upon. He also preached on occasion and was a support for Roberta in providing insight and a fresh perspective.

We often rode over to Sonlight for their evening devotionals, with David sometimes giving the lesson. We helped tutor the children, giving one-on-one attention and mentoring as we went along.

It was during the first year of our work at the Guest House that Roberta received the last three children who came to live with her.

Zachary, 17 months old, came a year after his buddy, Jonathan, and was just three months younger in age. After the earthquake, his mother lived in one of the tent cities which had become notoriously dangerous for women. This woman, especially vulnerable because of blindness, was raped and Zachary was born months later.

He was born with hydrocephalus, a condition in which one side of his brain does not process fluid adequately. Otherwise, he was healthy with no malaria, typhoid, or sores.

His blind mother did her best to take care of Zachary, but the toddler soon became an escape artist and she could not keep up with him. He is a strong-willed child and it may be that his stubbornness and a little bit of a mean streak kept him alive. One day he went missing and searchers found Zachary at the top of a tower. Zachary needed better supervision.

A Clay Jar Too Soon Broken

When he came to live at Sonlight, the only utterances he made were goat-like sounds which temporarily masked his smartness. He used his keen imagination to make a toy out of anything his little hands could find. Zach learned to sit in his chair during class time, listen well, and absorb what was taught. Roberta was especially impressed when he quickly learned his colors. He mirrored his little mentor, Jo-Jo, and followed him anywhere. The toddler was also a sleepwalker, giving his new mom more than one scare in the middle of the night.

In just a few months after Zachary arrived in 2013, Sarah made her appearance. The guard summoned Roberta to the gate and there stood Sarah. "I have nowhere to go, Mom." Sara was six years old and, like most Haitian children, was just a wisp of a child. She ate at the Nutrition Center, just like her mother before her. Sarah had essentially been abandoned by all her family members for several days. Though Sarah didn't know what to do, she knew a woman who did.

Six-month-old Macken was the last child to join the Sonlight family, coming shortly after Sarah. His mom abandoned him and the extended family rejected him because of a feud with his mom. One day, Wiles came walking into the yard with this "bundle of joy", his nephew Macken.

Wiles was ready to quit school to work so he could take care of him. Roberta said he couldn't quit school and the girls in the family said they couldn't let Macken die, which would have happened had they returned him. The dilemma was resolved when Michemana stepped up and accepted the responsibility of the baby's care. The family was now complete, though none of us realized it at the time.

All the while Roberta was busy settling new children into her home, she continued to mentor me in my new job. With Roberta's help and encouragement, I became more confident, and I also learned more and more about the person and life of Roberta . I reflected on the early days when I first met Roberta and how I just wanted to rub elbows with her in hopes that some of her faith would rub off on me. As the years went by, I learned about the toils, snares, and trials that molded her relationship with God. I wondered if my faith would have strengthen as hers did, or would it have crumbled?

Before Guest House days, I was puzzled by how much Roberta accomplished in a day's time. Now I began to realize how she did it: she arose by 5:00 in the morning and went to bed between 11:00 p.m. and 2:00 a.m., rarely stopping in between. When she did stop, her head could be seen slumped over as she slept, even while stopped in traffic; it's the truth! Working at the Guest House opened my eyes to the innumerable burdens she shouldered before and after our arrival. It pleased me more than I can say to ease one area in her life.

She was an encouraging teacher and cheerleader to me even though sometimes I felt like she coaxed and pushed me to the brink, only to disappear when I turned around searching for her reassurance. I would have grown up more self-assured had she been around in my childhood years.

There were days when Roberta needed a few minutes to just be still and our quarters at the Guest House were a respite for her --- a place to try to make sense of her crazy day as she sat in one of our comfortable recliners (thank you, Estes!) and savored the fan stirring the air. On rare occasions she would stop by for a hot shower. It was my pure joy to be there for her as she certainly was for me.

Before and after our tenure at the Guest House, Roberta and I kept in close contact. We used the internet and texting to stay in touch, often remembering with sadness earlier missionaries who were cut off from their family and friends without electronics, even as she had been in her early years in Haiti.

We also called often. Roberta talked about her recent challenges or day-brighteners with the children or maybe about her latest business adventure idea. Sometimes I just called to pray with her. Early each Sunday morning I emailed her a Scripture and shared what was going on in my life. If I missed a Sunday, I soon got a call to find out what was wrong. This routine was hard to break after her death.

We loved each other and working together tightened our bond. But no relationship is without issues and ours was no exception. One of the wonderful things about heaven is there will be no relationship problems. From the early days of our friendship, we both considered the work we felt called to do in Haiti to be of prime importance and our differences paled by comparison. When it is God's will you are seeking, it's easier to give up your own will. We worked through our personality quirks and our friendship was all the stronger.

Chapter 23
Sweet Memories

My heart is full of many sweet memories and funny stories. I've selected a few to share, in hopes one of them will bring you a chuckle and all will bring encouragement.

The first two stories occurred before my husband and I moved to Port-au-Prince.

On my very first trip to visit Roberta, a lady at worship asked if I was Roberta's mother. As Roberta translated, I just stared at Roberta in disbelief that such a question would be asked. What I didn't understand was that nationality transcended color. Because we were both Americans, it was possible I was her mother. That question stuck with me through the years and got me to thinking: we should all live with such a kindred faith that we look like family no matter our color.

****

The other memory from pre-Guest House days is the first and only time I felt in danger. When we were out and about in the city, Roberta and Thomas were always precautious, aware of their surroundings, and smart about knowing when to stay home. I always felt safe in their presence, wherever we were.

I felt safe the many years we slept behind double-locked doors with guard dogs in the yard and concrete walls topped with razor wire and cemented broken bottles. At Roberta's home, sometimes she had an armed guard when she could afford him.

Roberta

There was one exception. It was 2:00 a.m. and Roberta's voice rang out angrily and fearfully as she screamed, "Get out! Get out!" Sleeping with four of the girls in the downstairs bedroom, I was the only one immediately up and out of my bed. Thinking intruders were in the house, I had my hand on the doorknob to run help her. Then it occurred to me, with my white face I might make matters worse for her --- they could use me as a hostage. My hand went on and off that doorknob many times. Roberta kept using the same words and I never heard other voices.

Finally, quiet filled the house. After a few minutes, I opened the door, went to the stairs, and timidly called, "Roberta?" She blessedly came down. Someone had left the dogs inside at bedtime. They found, attacked, and killed Roberta's cat, her favorite mouser. She had been yelling at the dogs to get out.

I went back to my bed in a room full of sleeping girls.

****

Some of my "funnest" memories with Roberta were our trips half-way up the mountain to Petionville, where the big grocery stores were located. It was a two-hour trip due to heavy traffic and narrow, twisty roads filled with pedestrians who just knew you would stop before you hit them. On some of these trips, I thought about Roberta's story of walking the five miles up that mountain the day she decided to escape the stares and coldness of her ex-husband's family those many years ago.

These trips were a blast! Roberta drove over to pick me up and we enjoyed orange-cranberry scones or bacon and pancakes with hot tea; she was not a coffee drinker and never wanted to be close to an egg. With the monumental grocery list in hand after breakfast, we waved good-bye to Dave and

Ronaldo, drove through the gate, and headed out for our big adventure.

Because it took two or three times longer to get anywhere in Haiti than in the States, most of our visiting time was done in the truck, while running errands. As we bumped and jostled and fell in potholes, our teeth would sometimes rattle. Roberta knew how to laugh and make whatever task we were doing more fun. At one point the Kia had a starter problem and while I sat behind the wheel to start it, she was outside the truck holding the little "thingy" down or vice versa. We laughed as we both went to man our stations.

She talked and yelled over the noise of the truck as it crunched gravel and fellow drivers honked and screamed. Roberta vented and shared. I know many of you have enjoyed the same experience. That woman could talk!

Our first stop was the One Stop grocery to share a visit with the friendly father/son team who owned the store and cashed our checks --- and to get Roberta a cold Dr. Pepper!

She took a short cut as we continued up the mountain to the Caribbean grocery store (remember the buggy Snickers bar?), recently rebuilt after it was demolished by the earthquake. This route included a stop sign at a hard-right turn on a steep hill that had no protection from the drop-off beside the road. Her vehicles were big and had stick shifts. I always dreaded when the car stalled. Trying to get it re-started as it was backing down this hill was tricky and I helped by closing my eyes and mouth. She laughed all the while.

The Caribbean is the largest grocery store in Petionville with a close second just blocks away, named Giant. At the Caribbean, we had tasty pizza and yummy pastries in the newly built deli café before we shopped. It was cool and refreshing. We rationalized this practice by assuring ourselves we'd buy less groceries with full tummies.

We then went to Giant to find items the Caribbean did not have. Skinny loaves of hot, fresh baked French bread were their specialty as well as Roberta's favorite chocolate éclairs in the little bakery tucked away upstairs. We giggled like teenagers as we returned to the truck, broke into the goodies, and headed home. We left the grocers happy as we drove away with our $600 worth of food.

****

Tuesday, May 20, 2014, two days before the arrival of a 36-member Estes medical team, I began feeling weak, feverish, and achy. Meals were planned, food purchased, and the ground team at the Guest House on schedule. But the day before they arrived, with Roberta sitting beside me on the bed, I tearfully realized I had contracted Chikungunya; I was stuck in bed.

Chikungunya is a viral infection transmitted by mosquitoes, leaving the victim feverish with arthritic pains all over the body and extreme fatigue. The disease ran rampant through Haiti in 2014. My visiting brother, Charlie McGee, and Roberta ultimately contracted it, as well, and both had longer-lasting side effects than did I. Incidentally, through the years, Roberta also contracted numerous cases of malaria and typhoid, as do most missionaries living long-term in tropical climates.

My tears were for the burden placed on Roberta's shoulders. I had come to Haiti to host, so "all" she would have to do was provide transportation and translators, be on 24-hour-call troubleshooting, and generally hold everything together as she mothered her children around the corner and down the street.

God rescued us both with an unexpected passenger on the same flight with the medical team: Megan McIntyre. Megan has people skills, is an accomplished cook, and a great organizer. She stepped into somebody else's Haitian kitchen with 36 people to feed for a week and never missed a beat. Extraordinaire!

As I lay in bed that week, I listened to the sweet sounds of chatter and banter amongst the team, the clatter of meal preparations in the kitchen, and the beautiful singing in the evening devotionals outside my window. I was at peace.

****

Roberta hosted many, many visitors to Port au Prince, but she also encouraged and supported ministries in other parts of Haiti. In 2012 and 2014, my brother, Charlie, and his wife, Susan, spearheaded mission trips with their congregation located in St. Joseph, MI. They bought hundreds of pounds of rice and beans, brought clothes for children in an orphanage, and conducted a VBS in a tiny coastal church in Port de Paix, northern Haiti.

The long-distance outreach was incredibly difficult to plan, organize, and orchestrate, but you know our girl, Roberta, got the job done with extreme proficiency. She coordinated with the Michigan team and the Haitian preacher to purchase food and other supplies in Port au Prince to take to Port de Paix. It was an 8½-hour journey, one way, half of which was on unpaved roads in rural communities, sometimes no more than a cow path. Roberta dealt with vehicle breakdowns and blown tires along the way, the norm for trips of any significant length. She brought most of her family as translators and workers.

The second and last trip the St. Joseph group made was in December 2014 and this trip included the McGee's daughter, Heather Fisbeck, and grandson, Will, along with other church members. The team gladly gave up Christmas with their families to bring joy and love to Haiti. As Roberta, David, and I hosted the team at the Guest House, we all enjoyed their hugs, Christmas spirit, and gifts to Roberta's children.

Roberta

All the while Susan was fighting breast cancer. My sweet Susan died a month later, January 26th, on Roberta's birthday.

Mission Team from St. Joseph, MI
Charlie far left; Susan 4th from left

****

Ron and Dianna Cyphers were among the first Haitian missionaries we met. They managed the Cap Haitien Children's Home and, over the years, grew very dear to us. As they traveled frequently in and out of Haiti, they used our home in Palm Beach Gardens, FL, as their stop-over, sometimes for a week at a time. Roberta and the Cyphers were in the same line of work and had conversations about their respective roles and challenges of ministering to children who have no place else to go.

Ron is legally blind, a big teddy bear of a man, and Dianna is a tiny, feisty woman who had command of the Haitian roads when she was behind the wheel. They are not your usual couple. Ron and Dianna opened their home to troubled and mentally ill children for all their working years. In their sixties they "retired" to the Haitian orphanage and worked there until their health drove them back to their doctors in the States.

We enjoyed good food, much laughter, intricate puzzles, and old-fashioned conversation. They were an encouragement, an inspiration, and another testimony that God does not have a retirement plan. In their mid-70's, they are now living in California near their daughter, enjoying their view and each other as they fight Ron's cancer.

Ron and Dianna Cyphers

****

When there were no guests at the Guest House, we invited the kids over for supper and games (bingo was their favorite) and for special celebrations like birthdays and the Fourth of July. Roberta worked hard and she played hard. She knew how to have a good time, even on a tight budget, making exceptions for important things like fireworks. She did love her fireworks. She traveled all over Port-au-Prince trying to find them for the Fourth of July celebration, succeeding about half the time.

Hamburgers and Hot Dogs for July 4

Roberta was proud to be an American and loved her country; she cranked up Lee Greenwood as he sang, "Proud to be an American!" and sang along with him loudly in the courtyard. When everybody's tummies were full of hot dogs and watermelon, she took a couple of the bigger boys with her to the flat roof of the Guest House and lit the treasured fireworks. I cringed while the children squealed with delight.

****

Sometimes we had sleep-overs with the girls and supervised them as they cut veggies, seasoned tomato sauce, grated cheese, and made pizza dough. We played games or watched a movie and made popcorn. We tried a night with the boys, but they would rather stay home and eat rice and beans --- go figure.

Gooey Pizza Dough
Guerline & Michemana

****

One of the dearest times we experienced with the children was the last night of any given medical mission team's visit. Roberta and all the kids came over and enjoyed supper with us, followed by a devotional. 60 plus of us celebrated a week of hard work and sweet fellowship. The children loved all the extra playtime shared with the young people on the team.

****

Roberta returned to the States occasionally to make speeches, purchase fabric for the Dorcas Sisters, visit her parents, or check in with the Estes church. While she was gone on one such trip, she left us "newbies" on our own. My husband came down with malaria, of course.

As it turned out, we were in excellent hands of responsible young adults. David was too weak to walk and Francky came to help Ricardo carry him to the car and drive us to the hospital. We didn't know the language but fully trusted our guys. After a couple of hours spent in an admittance/examining area, the doctor started David's IV medications and determined David needed to stay the night. We knew from Roberta's previous experiences to ask for a private room. The boys helped us to our room and then headed home.

Around supper time, Francky and Achimetre returned with food Michemana had cooked for us. Since you must provide your own meals, they were welcomed sights. Being protective, Ricardo wanted to sleep in the car in the parking lot to be close to us, but was not allowed to do so. We settled in for the night.

The room was tiny. Do you ever wonder where those old hospital beds from the 1960's went? We found them, hand cranks and all. There was one small, high window and a tiny fan up near the ceiling. David was gracious enough to share his single bed with me and there we sweated for the rest of the night.

Morning rays came and so did our precious caretakers. Francky brought Guerline and I remember well

206

her broad smile as she handed us her homemade chocolate chip muffins for breakfast.

The doctor came in with a choice for us: stay longer and receive IV meds or go home and take them orally. Hmmm, no brainer there!

That hospital visit will always hold a dear place in our hearts. These young people were beautiful, responsible, and compassionate. When we later told Roberta her children made us feel safe and loved, she just grinned and said, "Of course they did."

****

Perhaps my favorite memory with Roberta occurred during the only time she visited in our home in St. Paul, MN. One morning while I was playing "You've Turned My Mourning into Dancing", she popped into the room, took me by the hand, and we danced and laughed and celebrated our friendship. I loved her. I loved her spontaneity, her confidence in finding another way when things went awry (often in Haiti), her genuine and unashamed love for the Father, her adventuresome spirit, and her love and dreams for her children.

****

I have a sweet kid-story. We went back to visit in July 2016, our first visit since Roberta's funeral. I mixed together a birthday cake for Guerline and put it in the oven. As I opened the door to the workroom to check on its progress, I saw the young son of Ketty and Martial Viciere. Kenley was sitting on his heels quietly and patiently looking at the cake through the darkened window of the oven as it baked, his face cradled in his hands. I turned the oven light on and got him a chair. It was probably the first time he had seen cake batter turn into something light and fluffy and yummy to eat. It's the little things in life we so often take for granted.

****

We took our grandson, Alex, on several trips with us. One day the three of us were in the car with Roberta, headed up the mountain, when we noticed the car in front of us suddenly moving backwards, coming straight toward us.   It was like one of those slow-motion movies --- you see the accident coming and there's not a thing you can do.

Our damaged car had to be towed. We were all sitting in the car when the tow truck backed up and hooked us up. With puzzled looks, we asked if we weren't supposed to get out of the car. "Stay in the car.", translated Roberta. Ten-year-old Alex thought that ride was the coolest thing ever --- he talked about it for weeks.

****

My last story occurred after Roberta's death. While my husband and I were in Haiti for her funeral, I taught the ladies' Sunday morning class, the same class I was privileged to teach while living there. The lesson was intended to help them understand the grief we were all sharing was just for the moment --- the best is yet to come. We struggle in this life for a short time, then we get to live in God's presence for eternity, free from pain and tears. Satan wants us to believe this grief is all there is. But we have hope and the best is yet to come.

A Clay Jar Too Soon Broken

To help them understand the message, I borrowed an idea from the past. I explained in America, after we have eaten our supper, we oftentimes will have desert. Sometimes a hostess will instruct her guests to "keep your fork; the best is yet to come!" (I had a bit of difficulty helping them understand this concept.)

But they got it and beamed brightly when I took silver forks out of my satchel and told them again, "The best is yet to come!" as I gave each woman her fork.

PART VII
Spurring One Another On
to Good Works

"Maybe I can't stop the downpour, but I can join you for a walk in the rain."
- Unknown

Chapter 24
Faithful Partners

I must mention some of the faithful friends whom Roberta loved and trusted and who partnered with her in ministries over the years before her death in 2015. They loved, encouraged, and offered help as they joined her for a walk in the rain together, shifting some of Roberta's load to their own shoulders. I'm sure there are other people upon whom Roberta relied and who loved her and supported her, though all these servants were not known to me.

Brothers Jean Claubert Belton, Felix Saint-Hubertand, and Beaubrun Origene were loyal friends she trusted and on whom she depended.

Brother Jean Claubert is the preacher of the Ganthier church (also known as the Bonnet church) where Roberta and the children worshipped. Through the years, Roberta taught Bible classes for the women and children. It was here that her boys learned to preach and her girls learned to teach. Close bonds were made as the church and the Sonlight Children's Home grew together in their relationships with one another. Today, Brother Jean Claubert continues to preach and plan events for the young people in the churches in their area and Sister Jean Claubert teaches the women and children.

Brother and Sister Felix, the preacher and his wife in nearby Cite Soleil, worked often with Roberta, hosting meetings and Ladies' Days. The three of them worked closely together as they explored and sought solutions for issues facing the church in Cite Soleil. They faithfully continue serving the church and its community.

Brother Beaubrun is a policeman and was there to help Roberta with many conflicts, advisements, and the expediting of various matters. Sister Beaubrun is a vital leader in the Dorcas Sisters of Haiti. Brother Beaubrun also works closely with Larry Waymire at the International School of Theology and with the new Sonlight house parents, Martial and Ketty Viciere, offering help or his expertise.

As previously mentioned, Eluide worked in Roberta's homeschool program for years. Because of her integrity and dependability, Roberta also gave Eluide the responsibility of paying the school fees for the children in the Nutrition Center as well as purchasing and delivering fabric to the seamstresses for their uniforms. Through the good years and the tough years, Eluide was a beloved, trusted helper to Roberta and today continues her faithful work at Sonlight.

For the past seven or eight years, Sylvia has been the mainstay in the kitchen and has watched over the little children with great patience and love. Roberta depended on her with complete trust. When she made her numerous trips to the States, Sylvia oftentimes brought her two sons and moved in with the children at Sonlight. After Roberta was killed, Marchodson and Sylvia were the glue that held things together until new caregivers were found. Sylvia continues to keep the kitchen running smoothly and supervises the younger children, who are fast growing older.

Marchodson ultimately finished his medical school coursework in St. Kitts and did very well. He completed his pre-med courses in a school located in Port-au-Prince. The school closed and his records have been lost. As a result, Marchodson, in his mid-20's at the writing of this book, has been unable to get into an internship or residency program to complete his doctorate.

Marchodson

Mona has risen before the sun for the past five years, preparing breakfast and lunch for the hungry children in the Nutrition Center, five days a week. She took the worry out of Roberta's day, in making sure the 150 children were fed on time before heading to school. On Friday afternoons, food packets from Feed My Starving Children, a non-profit group based in Minnesota, are given to the children so they and their families can eat over the weekend. Mona, punctual and dependable, continues in her same role today in the Nutrition Center.

Moises came to work for Roberta two or three years before her death. Having lived several years in the States, he is fluent in English and has a driver's license. With these skills, plus his attributes of integrity, a good work ethic, and a love for kids, Roberta thought him to be a good fit for the work --- and he was.

Roberta

Like Thomas, he was her "go to" person to fill in gaps. Much of the driving that had eaten up her time and energy was turned over to him. He handled large sums of money with utmost integrity, faithfully bringing receipts and change at the end of the day. Roberta felt completely at ease when she offered him the responsibility of driving the Nutrition Center kids to and from school. And there was a huge bonus: he could fix trucks and cars!

Moises was arrested for killing Roberta a few days after her death. Following a grueling two-month imprisonment in an over-populated jail cell plagued with rats, he was finally released. Moises returned to his hometown to live near relatives.

Martial and Ketty Viciere have partnered with Roberta after her death. When Roberta's life and dreams were taken from her, Ketty and Martial stepped in to raise the children she left behind.

Martial, Ketty and the Children

Martial and Ketty, with their 12-year-old daughter, Lithama, and ten-year-old son, Kenly, moved into the Sonlight Children's Home in January 2016, three months after Roberta's death. Martial attended the International School

216

of Theology and Larry Waymire recommended him as one of his top preaching students. He has a degree in psychology from a university in Haiti with experiences in various ministries, including ten years as a police officer.

Chapter 25
Haiti's Greatest Need:
Equipped Preachers

Roberta was an enthusiast for a school of preaching to be established in the Port-au-Prince area. She believed equipping men who want to be serious students of the Bible was the greatest need of the Lord's church --- the only way to enable His church to grow strong and healthy. They needed a preachers' school.

Larry Waymire, who helped with the earthquake recovery, spearheaded the effort. The International School of Theology (IST) was established in Port-au-Prince under the sponsorship of the Bear Valley Bible Institute in Colorado and Freed-Hardeman University. The following is Larry's short history of how conversations between himself and Roberta transformed a need into a reality.

> "After I had been working in Haiti for about a year, Roberta and I started discussing the need for a school of preaching. Through Roberta's connections with various congregations, she could see a need for additional training for many of the preachers. While most were doing the best they could, they were limited by education and tools for study. When we had the preacher/elder conferences, I asked what

was the greatest need for the church and they said the same thing, 'We need a way to train preachers.'

"When the discussion first started, the earthquake relief was full force, so it had to be put on the back burner. About the third year, as the relief effort was beginning to slowdown, we started planning again. I asked Roberta who she thought would be good, honest men on whom I could depend. These men would serve as the local directors and I would have to depend heavily on them.

"She said brothers St. Hurbert Felix and Origen Beaubrun were who she would pick. So, as I started planning for the school, I met with them along with Roberta to discuss their willingness to serve. They both agreed to work with us as we started planning for the school. I told them, 'This is to be a labor of love because we have no money.' They both agreed to serve without pay or compensation.

"As time moved forward, a date was set to start the school in August of 2013. We needed a place to meet so Roberta and I began simply driving around and looking for a location. We looked at one and made an offer but they never called us back. We passed a large three-story building and Roberta said, 'That building looks like it may have some empty space.' So we stopped and spoke to the guard and he gave us a phone number to call as we looked inside. It met all our needs so we rented the location. This I believe took place in early 2013.

"The rent was $1,250 per month and a year's rent had to be paid in advance. I had zero dollars at the time but we agreed to rent the facility. While we did not know where the funds were, God did. We met at this location for two years and graduated twenty-four students in May 2016. On several occasions during the two-year period, Roberta prepared meals for the students and often picked up the American teacher and prepared meals for the students and directors. When we had conferences, she would often prepare meals for the entire group which could be as many as sixty-five people.

"As time went on, Roberta and I dreamed together of how we could expand on the idea of the school, plant a congregation, and develop a camp area for churches to use. One day Roberta called and said, 'I think I have found a location that might serve all of our needs.' The same man who had handled the purchase of the home for the children, and I believe the guest house, was also the person handling the sale of the property at La Tremblay 12, #7. It was in June of 2015 that we first looked at the property. Roberta helped contact a notary who would do the research and make sure we could buy the property legally. Roberta, I believe, had used him before for other legal matters. She and I made several trips to the property and dreamed of how it would look and what we could accomplish together if we bought the property.

"On October 10, 2015, she was taken from us and would not see the completion of our dream. Yet, in February of 2016, the sale was approved and we began work immediately. First, we had to rebuild the front wall and make repairs to the house which was already on the property. After that was completed, Brother Beaubrun and his family moved in to help secure the property. Second, the first classroom was constructed and in August of 2016 our first class met at our new location. Third, in January of 2017 we were able to construct a wall that would enclose one half of the property. We will enclose the backside of the property in the future. Our next phase is to complete the construction of the school building. When finished, it will be about 5,600 sq. feet, have three large classrooms, two offices, a

221

Roberta

room for visiting teachers, two restrooms, a storage facility, and a kitchen. The present classroom which is about 850 sq. feet will serve as a media center where we will offer online classes. In the distant future, our dream includes a satellite school in each of the remaining districts.

"This all started with a conversation while traveling the bumpy roads of Santo and dreaming about how to strengthen the churches, equip the preachers, and expand the borders of God's kingdom."

Larry Waymire

Education can change a life, -
Bobbie Solley

Chapter 26
Hand Grasping Hand
Across an Ocean

"I have never let my schooling interfere with my education."
Mark Twain

Somehow this quote reminds me of Bobbie Solley and, as she tells her story, those of you who know her might agree with me.

This is a story of the hand of one woman living in the United States grasping the hand of another woman living in Haiti to initiate change in the education of children in this third world country.

Bobbie shares with us how she and Madeline, a Haitian schoolteacher, connected and began to change the way Haitian teachers teach their students. This was the beginning of Roberta's dream to give not only her children a sound education, but all the children of Haiti. In the process, Roberta influenced Bobbie's life as Bobbie was challenged physically, mentally, and spiritually while learning to serve in this third world country.

"I met Roberta for the first time in 2011 at Healing Hands International's (HHI) Women of Hope conference in Nashville, TN. That year she received the Woman of the Year award and after listening to her speak, I knew why. I was blown away with what she had dedicated her life to do. I was amazed at the lives she was shaping and changing and I was stunned at the fact that she was doing it alone.

"I was a professor at Middle Tennessee State University at the time and had become extremely dissatisfied with my career and my life in general. The department where I worked was becoming increasingly toxic and unhealthy. The year before, my niece, Katie Frazier, and her husband, Shawn, and I had begun a prayer vigil asking God to open doors for me in the next five years so that I could retire from MTSU by the age of sixty.

"Throughout the summer of 2011, I continued to think about Roberta and her life choices and compared them with mine. I loved teaching but I began to wonder what else was out there for me. In February 2012, I once again attended the Women of Hope Conference. Roberta wasn't there that year but her name was everywhere. I had, by this time, met more people who worked at HHI and was told that the non-profit was looking to move into education. They were looking into the idea of going into Haiti to train teachers. Really???

"Two weeks later I met with a man from HHI who worked in Haiti quite a bit. We talked through all the possibilities. Two weeks after that I met with the president, vice-president, and development officer of HHI. Three weeks after that I made my first trip to Haiti.

"I had never been on a mission trip, never been to a third world country, never seen poverty like I saw, never been so moved in my whole life. I spent some time with Roberta at her house and was amazed at what she did and how she went about her day. I came back a changed woman. Through the prayers of Katie, Shawn, and I, we were convinced that God had opened a door He intended for me to go through now rather than to wait for five years when I was sixty. So, in May 2012 I retired from MTSU. I joined HHI in June and made my first trip with teachers in July of 2012. Our goal --- teach teachers in Haiti how to teach literacy to their students.

"From July 2012 to October 2015 I made twenty-one trips to Haiti to work with teachers. I thought I knew exactly what to do. After all, I had trained teachers my whole career; what could be so hard about doing it in Haiti? A lot!!! I quickly found out that I knew nothing. I knew nothing about the culture of Haiti, nothing about teachers in Haiti, nothing about children in Haiti, nothing about curriculum, nothing about schools. I knew absolutely nothing!!

"I had grand plans and ideas for us, nonetheless. We would show teachers how to teach their children to read and really comprehend, how to read aloud to their students, and how to help children become writers. All those plans went up in smoke on the very first day of the very first trip when we discovered there was no term for 'literacy' in Creole, there were no books to read aloud, and there was no paper and pencils for children to write with.

"That first trip Roberta was not involved with us other than to prepare lunch for us on Sunday. But as my visits became more frequent, I began to know Roberta, love Roberta, and rely on Roberta a great deal. Even after that first fiasco trip, I still knew nothing of what I needed to do and I'm sure, looking back, Roberta must have had a really good laugh at not only my sheer inability to grasp the whole concept of education in Haiti, but also at my arrogance and my pride.

225

Roberta

"While I was able to regroup on that first trip, teaching teachers in Haiti was something that would take every ounce of knowledge I currently had, plus a whole lot more that I didn't have. It would take listening to Roberta, the principals, the administrators of the schools, and to the teachers themselves before I could really develop a plan that even came close to working. It would take coming off of my own arrogance and pride. It would take recognizing that I had no answers and, most of all, it would take recognizing that God had the plan and He was going to work that plan no matter what I did.

"Many mistakes were made before I made the connections necessary to make something work. We failed a lot more than we succeeded at first and the whole time Roberta was my biggest cheerleader. She guided me through the hard, difficult days when nothing seemed to work. She celebrated with me when the small successes came. It didn't matter how small the success, it was counted as just that --- a success. Roberta coached me on how to talk with Haitians. She taught me how to settle conflict with the teachers. She showed me how to cut my losses and move on when circumstances became unfixable.

"But Roberta taught me so much more. She taught me what it meant to be a servant, a true servant of God. She taught me what humility looked like, what it acted like, and how it worked. She taught me when to stand up and fight and when to sit down and be quiet. She taught me what it meant to truly be a Christ-follower. She lived these things every single day of her life.

"And through the things she taught me about Christ, our work with teachers and schools slowly began to change. She would have to remind me from time-to-time, but I began letting God make the plans and lead me where He needed me to go. I learned to wait on

226

Him to show me what and how and with whom I needed to work. I also allowed Him to show me the American teachers who needed to go with me each visit. He knew better than anyone who would be needed and what they would be needed for and I let myself be led. Arrogance was replaced with humility. Pride was replaced with meekness. Trusting myself was replaced with trusting in God and in Him alone.

"Over the course of the three and a half years I worked in Haiti, we worked with over a hundred teachers in six different schools. It was Roberta who chose the schools we worked in and it was Roberta who handled all the logistical work that had to done before we arrived. It was Roberta who always had translators for us and it was Roberta who got us from place to place. In 2013 we began holding seminars for the teachers at Roberta's home.

"Teachers from five schools would come on a Saturday morning and sit through a hot, Haitian day in order to learn about what it meant to really teach a child to read. These seminars were instrumental in the change that began to take place in the schools. Teachers began putting into practice the things we were teaching and showing. They began to ask questions and became hungry for more. They became more willing to try new things and they became more willing to make mistakes in order to learn from them.

"My goal had always been to eventually turn the teaching of teachers over to Haitian teachers. Both Roberta and I believed that the biggest difference would be made if Haitians taught Haitians. So, in 2014 we began looking for an outstanding Haitian teacher who could continue to lead the teachers during the time span when I couldn't be there. Again God, through Roberta, led us to Madeline Joseph.

227

Roberta

"Madeline was one of the best and brightest teachers I had seen and in 2015 we hired her to be the liaison between the teachers and me. We were then working primarily with four schools. We really began to dig in with these teachers and principals and really saw a change in their attitudes and in their teaching. We continued to hold regular seminars when we were there and then Madeline would go into the classrooms to further support the learning the teachers had done.

"The education work in Haiti goes on. Madeline is doing a great job teaching and supporting teachers. We have hired another teacher, Bernadette St. Hubert, who does the same work as Madeline. I communicate with them via Go-to-Meeting and Skype. I have returned once since Roberta's death and plan on going again in August 2018. My time there is spent differently now, but the work that God started through Roberta and I will continue."

Bobbie Solley and Roberta

Part VIII
Saying Goodbye

"The Reason it hurts so much to separate is because our souls are connected."

Nicholas Sparks, The Notebook

Chapter 27
Roberta's Last Night

"He Heals the Brokenhearted and Binds Up Their Wounds."

Psalm 147:3

After I got Jan Sharp's 9:00 p.m. phone call the night Roberta was murdered, I looked at my husband and said, "She's not tired anymore."

On October 10, 2015, the Guest House was filled to overflowing, happy chatter and banter filling every corner. Not only was a large medical mission team staying at the house, but Bobbie Solley and her teachers were there, also. It was a Saturday night; the work of both teams had gone very well and folks were energized even though they were physically exhausted.

Roberta left around 8:30 p.m., drove home, and picked up three of her children to go with her to the gas station,

Roberta

ensuring there was plenty of gas in the vehicle for Sunday morning. They left their gate and had gone less than a quarter of a mile on the narrow road when a speeding vehicle passed and pulled in front of them, blocking Roberta's vehicle. An armed gunman stepped out and approached her window. As Roberta scrambled for her gun, he shot her seven times, killing her instantly. Taking four-year-old Jonathan (Jo-Jo) with him, he fled the scene, leaving Ben and Lofane trembling and stunned.

The two boys ran home to report what happened. Thomas was first on the scene. Over two years later, five people have been arrested, one of whom has been released and none have been convicted to my knowledge.

A couple of months after the event, an investigating official made a statement that Jonathan was alive and well, but no one has seen or heard from him.

Roberta and Jonathan (aka Jo-Jo)

A Clay Jar Too Soon Broken

Bobbie Solley graciously shares with us her account of that fateful night:

"On the weekend of Oct. 10, 2015, we had just completed one of the best trips we had ever had. Teachers in the schools were doing an outstanding job. By this time, every school had between 75-100 picture books at their disposal. They had the supplies they needed and they wowed us with their understanding of the concepts of reading and how they were implementing them. On Saturday, October 10, we held a fabulous seminar at Roberta's. We had over 45 teachers in attendance that day and the learning that took place could only be described as miraculous. God was present that day, as He was at everything we did, but it seemed as if that day it all came together. Madeline did an outstanding job teaching; she truly became the leader that day. It was a magical day, to say the least.

"The guest house where we stayed was full to overflowing that night. A medical team from Estes Church in Henderson, TN, arrived and together with our entire group, there were 38 people staying there. Roberta had cooked a special meal for our group and served it on the roof of the guest house where trees shaded us and a cool breeze blew over us. We sang with the whole group and prayed while Roberta left to go get boxes of dolls, aprons, and bags that the sewing ladies had made. It was a mad-house when she returned. Jo-Jo was in rare form and so was I. I got him all stirred up and Roberta had to tell both of us to calm down. The whole day had just been a blessing from God.

"Roberta left around 8:30. All the teachers who were with me, 10 in all, went upstairs to our very full bunk room to get ready for bed. I put my earplugs in, as usual, and lights went out relatively early. It felt like the middle of the night, but it was only shortly after

233

Roberta

10:30, I was awakened by someone touching my arm. I looked up and it was Roberta standing there. She said I needed to come downstairs with her. I tried to argue with her and she insisted that I put on shorts and come downstairs. I asked her if something had happened and she took me by the arm and led me down the stairs. At the bottom of the stairs, I turned to look at her again and Roberta was gone but Kathy Williams was standing there. God blessed me by sending Roberta back to help me down the stairs, but he allowed Kathy to give me the news. 'Bobbie, it's Roberta. She's dead.' My mind didn't compute what I was hearing. 'She's been murdered.'

"The rest of the night is somewhat of a blur to me. Before we woke up everyone, a small group of us stood around the table holding hands and prayed. One phrase I remember Frank saying many times, 'Lord, come quickly'. We had no idea what was going on and why Roberta, of all people, would have been murdered. Was someone out to get all Americans? After all, there were a lot of us there at the time. We just didn't know. Prayers continued as we thanked God for His perfect plan (even though we certainly didn't understand it that night). The one thing we could not do was stand around idle. Even though I was in shock, things had to be done. I thank God Rita Cochrane had arrived the day before. She worked with me at Healing Hands and helped me navigate the rough terrain of what had to be done. We had to wake up our team to tell them the news, which was so very difficult. But there were so many hard things that had to be done during those early morning hours they all began to run together.

"Phone calls home to loved ones had to be made quickly because social media had picked up the story by 1:00 AM. The next order of business was to get us out of the country. Flights had to be changed; I insisted that my entire group leave together.

234

Between Rita and I, we made all the necessary arrangements and at 6:00 am, all 10 of us plus two women from Estes, left the guest house with armed guards and attack dogs."

The guests at the Guest House were reeling with the news of Roberta's shocking death. Down the street and around the corner, the big green house held a family of about 18 children who just lost their mother, their only parent. As usual, Thomas carried his family and community through another tragic event.

People saw Roberta as someone who could save them. The night she was killed, the whole community came out with hundreds of people on the streets, crying, "Who will save my kids?" People came from Port au Prince the next day to find out what happened. Many just set up camp at the gate.

Mike, Daniel, Joseph, Micah, and Luke were puzzled each day why Mom didn't come home. When Mike finally asked, "When is Mom coming home?", he was answered, "Mom is not coming home."

Chapter 28
Remembering Roberta

Grateful hearts all over the world, from a little barefooted boy walking the rocky dirt streets of Santo, to a large publishing company, have paid tribute to Roberta during the last four years since her death October 10, 2015. Here are the words of friends, colleagues, and fellow workers sharing the profound influence Roberta had on their lives.

In the January/February 2010 issue of Christian Woman magazine, Roberta was featured on the front cover. Here is an excerpt from the inside article:

> "Roberta's energy and commitment make it easy for us to be involved in missions in Haiti. It really is a case of ministry emerging out of a combination of talents and opportunities. Her desire to be evangelistic, her love for children, and her organizational ability are seeds that have found fertile soil in Haiti and the Lord has been faithful to provide the increase! Providing a haven for starving, and/or abused children is obviously a good work in and of itself."

Debbie
Bumbalough
Vice President of Sales
Gospel Advocate
Written for "Christian Woman"
January/February issue, 2010.

Roberta

God's work in Santo, Haiti, using Roberta as one of His instruments, seemed to be at its pinnacle when the earthquake occurred a mere week after this issue was published. Natural disasters happen all over this world and we all suffer as a result. But it's also true that Satan is never happy when things are going well in God's kingdom and soon he is on the attack, "seeking whom he may devour". Roberta always felt like Satan had a very real presence in this disaster.

The next year, in 2011, Roberta was named "Woman of Hope" at the annual Women of Hope conference in Nashville, TN, hosted by Healing Hands International. In her keynote speech, Roberta shared with the audience many trials suffered and victories won during the first year following the earthquake.

The following are quotes from those who knew and loved Roberta:

The elders of the Estes Church of Christ; Henderson, TN:

"It is our intention to honor her memory by continuing the battle against Satan in Haiti and pressing on in the work of God's kingdom."

Widlord Thomas, Roberta's oldest son; Paris, TX:

"She took care of us until her last breath."

Michemana Blaise, one of Roberta's older girls; recent graduate of Freed-Hardeman University, Henderson, TN:

"I am so glad I got to know her; I would have missed out on one of the greatest women who walked on this earth."

A Clay Jar Too Soon Broken

Linda Lingo, friend; Tallahassee, FL:

"Roberta's life truly was one of light. Her light still shines today exposing the darkness of the world we live in and exposing the goodness of a God who truly loves us and wants us to be His children. Her life is an example of the power of God and how He can use us to further His kingdom if we dare to say 'YES' to Him. Roberta's life, her ministry, and her death all reflect one powerful testimony, 'God is enough'. Roberta, a woman truly worthy of praise."

Thoughts written by Linda for Roberta at the Women of Hope Conference in 2011:

"R - Roberta a beautiful woman of God

O – Outstanding in her dedication to God and His children

B – Believes that all things are possible thru God

E – Enjoys her life and her responsibilities

R – Rejoices in all circumstances of life

T – Trusts God completely to meet all her needs

A – A living example of how God's presence and power are enough"

Cecil May, Jr, Dean Emeritus of the Bible Department, Falkner University; Montgomery, AL:

"Roberta, though an American citizen, was most 'at home' in Haiti, especially when surrounded by otherwise homeless and hungry children. I met her through my brother, David, and his wife, Charlene, longtime volunteer missionaries to Haiti, when I

Roberta

accompanied them on a mission trip. Roberta had twenty or so, as she called them, 'her kids." living with her. She fed, clothed, mothered, and taught them the Bible, a good work ethic, and reading, writing, and arithmetic. They were 'her children', and she was obviously 'their Mother.' In addition, on weekdays, she had 150 or more children who came for breakfast and lunch, school lessons, and Bible lessons. She loved her Lord, her children, and all needy children. Many Haitian children will be in heaven because she loved, nurtured, and taught them."

David May, friend, fellow worker by her side, and author of "Out of the Pews and Into the Streets" (amazon.com/author/davidmay), and four other books; St. Paul, MN:

"When I first met Roberta, very briefly, in Port-au-Prince in 2001, I could hardly wait to get home to tell Charlene that I had just met the most amazing woman I had ever met in my lifetime, and I had known some pretty awesome women.

"Year by year of knowing Roberta after that --- fourteen years until she was murdered --- the impression grew stronger, not weaker. Her logo was 'God will provide' and she lived by that right down to something to put on the table for her kids to eat tonight. We met her before the ongoing support for her and her kids materialized and her faith was the most real, most material of anyone I knew or had read about. Charlene and I had studied Mother Theresa's life shortly before and I had just met her western parallel.

"I don't pretend to know why she was taken when she was, but I like the theory I heard someone put forward: that God decided she had done enough and decided to call her home to her reward, so he called off the angels He had assigned to guard her all those years.

"Roberta, we love you still and we thank you for the example you set for us all, an example we will not live up to, but one that will pull us all closer to being the servant the Lord deserves. May you rest in peace."

Jesse Robertson, friend, co-worker, and Professor of Bible at Harding University, Searcy, AR:

"Roberta is the only person I ever heard of that had four funerals. One in Haiti, one in Alabama, one in Tennessee and one in North Carolina. Our best estimate is that she was a foster mom to 60 children over the course of that ministry and Sonlight Children's Home continues to flourish under the stewardship of new houseparents. But how can you count the impact of such a life? Children fed, educated, and discipled. Widows helped. Churches encouraged. Campaigners inspired. New congregations involved in new mission works of their own. What a legacy!"

Connie Pritchard, friend, Learning Center Coordinator at Freed-Hardeman University, Henderson, TN:

"Roberta and I met in Haiti in May of 2010. Immediately, we bonded and were 'soul sisters'. She had a servant heart, a loving, welcoming smile, and a selfless attitude. Roberta had a positive, faith-filled outlook on life and loved and trusted God completely in all things. I miss her and the short time we resided together at 202 Seventh St., Henderson,

241

Roberta

TN. I owe my improved outlook on all things, spiritual and non-spiritual, to Roberta and the life she lived in serving God."

Megan McIntyre, friend and co-worker; Dickson, TN:

"Roberta. What a story to tell. A great friend, awesome mom, and amazing Christian woman. We became family. We connected. She encouraged me to read my Bible and learn more about our loving God.

"She was my encourager, my go-to for advice, my yelling post when I was angry, my shoulder to cry on, and my answer to so many questions I had while in Haiti.

"I remember cooking with her in her kitchen and making sure I had frozen Country Time Lemonade daily for her as she stopped by the Guest House or to hand it to her as she passed at the gate. I remember delivering supplies and food to orphanages and the looks on all the faces when we got there.

"One last thing --- was she perfect? No, but she was perfect enough for me."

Brother Jean Claubert Belton, friend and co-worker, preacher in Bonnet, Haiti (also known as Ganthier):

"I was blessed by her in so many ways. In 1999, my wife was pregnant; we had no job, no money even to see a Doctor. She has visited my wife one day and gave money to her to see the Doctor. Everything I own today comes from Roberta .

"She helped me find job and opened so many doors for me. She gave me a lot of contact like New Hope

Haiti Mission where I have got my first job. Estes, Healing Hands, etc....."

Edouard Ronaldo, grew up eating in the Nutrition Center and was hired a few years ago by Roberta to take care of the Guest House, Santo, Haiti:

> "Mom Roberta!!! I will never be able to forget you in my mind --- every time I think of you, tears run down from my eyes. I was a child under your care since 5 years of age, you put me in school, you helped me reading many things in my life. You taught me to work, you gave me good table manners, gave me wonderful gardening tips. You taught me how to care for animals. I have been taught by you how to cook and I have good English.

> "One day Mom Roberta cooked a meal for American guests, Miss Solley and Mrs. Purvis. When Mom told me food is ready, I came and Mom asked me to lead the table. I said this prayer: 'Let's pray. Thank you God for all you have done for us. I ask that you blessings be on Mom, bless this meal, and bless these people we have here with us. Father, it is in the Jesus name we pray you. Amen!!'

> "As soon as the prayer was finished Mom said to me, 'Oh!! Good job darling, you said everything just right.' For you see I had said the prayer in English. Who would have guessed? She hugged me and the American guests were happy for me also, since I had to put lots of effort into the prayer."

Sylvia Philisnor, friend and helper in the Sonlight Children's Home; Santo, Haiti:

> "I have met Roberta in 2007. She has invited me to come to church. I heard the gospel and get baptized

243

Roberta

for remission of my sins. After a while I have got a job from her. I have 2 kids, she always paid for their school and helped take good care of them. When I heard about Roberta's death, I could not stand. I am an orphan now because I lost my Mom. When Roberta was alive I have never got problem paying school for my kids. I will never forget Roberta."

Sylvia and Me
"The Best is Yet to Come"

Mona Louis, friend and cook for the Nutrition Center, Santo, Haiti:

"Roberta was a mother for me. Her death has a lot of consequences on my life because I still can't believe it's real. She was always ready to help those who are in needs and pray for people. Roberta always advised me about what to do in this life to remain a good servant of God. She never stopped saying: 'We're praying.' Roberta died indeed but her work still alive. I believe that I will see her again in heaven if I work in the nice way for the Lord as she did."

Mona and Bro. Jean Claubert

Eluide Gustinvil, friend, helper in Roberta's homeschool and in many other ways; Santo, Haiti:

Roberta

Eluide
(Said with tears in her eyes)

"Roberta was a flesh mother for me and my best friend ever. We had been working together for 12 twelve years and never got problem one day, which is unusual as human. She's never kept anything secret from me. She had a lot of respect for me and I had a lot of respect for her also. My Mom died and I will never find one like her. Roberta's death left tears in my eyes and sadness in my heart. She died but her work remain a testimony for everybody here. May her soul rest in peace!!"

EPILOGUE

On January 18, 2017, Jesse Robertson shared the life of Roberta in a chapel speech at Harding University in Searcy, AR, where he now teaches. In that talk, he included these thoughts by Theodore Roosevelt:

> "It is not the critic who counts; not the man who points out how the strong man stumbles, or where the doer of deeds could have done them better. The credit belongs to the man who is actually in the arena, whose face is marred by dust, and sweat, and blood; who strives valiantly; who errs, who comes short again and again, because there is no effort without error and shortcoming; but who does actually strive to do the deeds; who knows great enthusiasms, the great devotions; who spends himself in a worthy cause; who at the best knows in the end the triumph of high achievement, and who at the worst, if he fails, at least fails while daring greatly, so that his place shall never be with those cold and timid souls who neither know victory nor defeat."

Jesse then gave his own call to arms to shine Jesus' light in Satan's darkness:

"Holding up your light in a dark corner of the world is not for the faint-hearted or the uncommitted. It is for those who are willing to risk failing in the hope that God will use your weakness to show his strength. Not everyone is cut out to work in Haiti, or similarly harsh environments, but some are. More to the point, however, what if each of us determined to

Roberta

find our own dark corner and tenaciously shine our lights? +What if we gave up on the income dreams and plans for a comfortable life and decided that with God's help we would make sure that all the days of our lives added up to something greater?"

"Roberta's death was tragic, but I am so glad that her life was not. She did not wonder if she was living for Jesus. Can you imagine the joy that infuses the life of a person who gets up every day knowing that they are doing what Jesus wants them to do? Help the fatherless and the widows. CHECK! Give to those who ask from you. CHECK! I was hungry and you visited me; I was thirsty and you gave me drink; I was naked and you clothed me. CHECK! CHECK! CHECK!

"Fear did not cause her to bury her talent and it is not hard to imagine hearing the Lord say, 'Well done, you good and faithful servant. Enter into the joys of your Lord.'

"My candle burns at both ends;

It will not last the night;

But ah, my foes, oh, my friends ---

It gives a lovely light!"

- Edna St. Vincent Millay

Made in the USA
Monee, IL
13 February 2020